W9-BOO-506

CARIBBEAN SEA

ATLANTIC OCEAN

Gulf of Honduras

Lake of Nicaragua

CENTRAL AMERICA

PUNTA DE GALLINAS

Barranquilla
Cartagena

Panama

Golfo del Darién

Medellín BOGOTÁ
COLOMBIA
17 100
Nevado del Ruiz

QUITO
ECUADOR
Cotopaxi 19 347
Guayaquil
Golfo de Guayaquil

ARCHIPIÉLAGO DE COLÓN (GALÁPAGOS ISLANDS) (Ec.)

ISLA DE MALPELO (Colombia)

DEL COCO (Costa Rica)

Maracaibo La Guaira
Valencia CARACAS
VENEZUELA
Mérida Ciudad Bolívar Orinoco
Cerro Icutú 7800

Boa Vista do Rio Branco
GUIANA HIGHLANDS

Georgetown Paramaribo
GUYANA SURINAME FR. GUIANA
Cayenne

BARBADOS
TRINIDAD AND TOBAGO
Port of Spain

Chiclayo
Trujillo
Nevado Huascarán 22 205

Chimbote

LIMA
Callao

PERU
Iquitos Leticia

Rio Negro
Japurá
Putumayo
Manaus (Manáos)
Rio Solimões (Amazonas)
Rio Amazonas

Belém (Pará)
ILHA DE MARAJÓ
Equator

São Luís (Maranhão)

ROCEDOS SÃO PEDRO E SÃO PAULO (Brazil)

Fortaleza (Ceará)
CABO DE SÃO ROQUE
Natal
João Pessoa (Paraíba)
RECIFE (Pernambuco)
Maceió

ARQUIPÉLAGO FERNANDO DE NORONHA (Brazil)

Arequipa
Volcán Misti 19 098
Mollendo

Cuzco

La Paz
Nev. Illimani 21 201
BOLIVIA
Sucre
Potosí

ATACAMA

Iquique

Antofagasta
Taltal

ISLA DE SAN FELIX (Chile) ISLA DE SAN AMBROSIO (Chile)

B R A Z I L

CHAPADA DE MATO GROSSO
Cuiabá

Brasília

Diamantina
Pico da Bandeira 9482
Belo Horizonte
Vitória
CABO FRIO

Salvador (Bahia)

SERRA DO ESPINHAÇO

BRAZIL HIGHLANDS

Rio de Janeiro
Santos
RIO DE JANEIRO

Florianópolis

Salta
Tucumán
GRAN CHACO
PARAGUAY
Asunción
Corrientes

SÃO PAULO

Tropic of Capricorn

Copiapó

Coquimbo

Valparaíso
SANTIAGO
Concepción

ISLAS DE JUAN FERNÁNDEZ (Chile)

Córdoba
Mendoza
Rosario
Santa Fe
Salto
URUGUAY
Rio Grande
Pôrto Alegre

A R G E N T I N A

Santa Fe
BUENOS AIRES MONTEVIDEO
La Plata
Rio de la Plata
PAMPAS

Bahía Blanca

Valdivia

Puerto Montt
ISLA DE CHILOÉ

ARCHIPIÉLAGO DE LOS CHONOS

Viedma
Golfo San Matías

Comodoro Rivadavia
Golfo San Jorge

Monte Valentín 13 314

WELLINGTON
HANOVER

DESOLACIÓN

Río Gallegos
Estrecho de Magallanes
Punta Arenas
TIERRA DEL FUEGO
MT. DARWIN 8700
ISLA DE LOS ESTADOS
CABO DE HORNOS (CAPE HORN)

FALKLAND IS. (ISLAS MALVINAS) (Br.)
Stanley

Drake Passage

Antarctic Circle

SOUTH GEORGIA (Falkland Is.)

SOUTH SANDWICH IS. (Falkland Is.)

SOUTH ORKNEY IS. (B.A.T.)

SOUTH SHETLAND ISLANDS (B.A.T.)

JOINVILLE

SOUTH GREENWICH MERIDIAN

JAMES ROSS
ROSS

ATLANTIC OCEAN

PACIFIC OCEAN

Scale 1:40 000 000; one inch to 630 miles
Lambert's Azimuthal Equal Area Projection
Elevations and depressions are given in feet

Miles	200	400	600	800	1000
Kilometers	400	800	1200	1600	

Longitude West of Greenwich

copyright by Rand McNally & Co., 84-S-18

Goode's World Atlas ©1991 by Rand McNally R.L. 91-S-251

Relief

Meters		Feet
3050		10 000
1525		5000
610		2000
305		1000
0	Sea Level	0
152.5		500
1525		5000
3050		10 000
6100		20 000

Enchantment of the World

URUGUAY

By Marion Morrison

Consultant for Uruguay: George I. Blanksten, Ph.D., Professor Emeritus of Political Science, Northwestern University, Evanston, Illinois

Consultant for Reading: Robert L. Hillerich, Ph.D., Visiting Professor, University of South Florida; Consultant, Pinellas County Schools, Florida

CHILDRENS PRESS®

CHICAGO

GALLINAS SCHOOL LIBRARY
177 N. San Pedro Road
San Rafael CA 94903

Vintage cars, called cachilas, *are used for everyday transportation.*

Project Editor: Mary Reidy
Design: Margrit Fiddle

Library of Congress Cataloging-in-Publication Data

Morrison, Marion.
    Uruguay / by Marion Morrison.
        p.   cm. — (Enchantment of the world)
    Includes index.
    Summary: Presents a history of a small South American
country, discussing its people, everyday and cultural life,
and problems.
    ISBN 0-516-02607-0
    1. Uruguay—Description and travel—1981—Juvenile
literature.   2. Uruguay—History—Juvenile
literature.   [1. Uruguay.]   I. Title.   II. Series.
F2708.5.M673   1992   91-35144
989.5—dc20   CIP
                                                        AC

Copyright © 1992 by Childrens Press®, Inc.
All rights reserved. Published simultaneously in Canada.
Printed in the United States of America.
    3 4 5 6 7 8 9 10 R 01 00 99 98 97

Picture Acknowledgments
AP/Wide World Photos: 49, 87, 90 (left)
Art Museum of the Americas: 89 (left and right)
The Bettmann Archive: 40 (right), 42, 62

© Cameramann International, Ltd.: 4, 69 (2 photos), 70
(top right), 71 (bottom), 74 (left), 76, 77 (right), 113 (top
right and bottom left)
Historical Pictures Service: 30, 40 (left)
North Wind Picture Archives: 43
Chip and Rosa Maria de la Cueva Peterson: 63 (right), 101
Photri: 13, 64, 66 (top), 78, 115
Reuters/Bettmann: 52 (2 photos), 53
Root Resources: © **Alan G. Nelson,** 21 (left); © **Jane P.**
Downton, 24, 91, 113 (bottom right)
South American Pictures: © **Tony Morrison,** Cover, 2
cover insets, 5, 6, 8, 10, 11, 12, 15, 16, 19 (2 photos), 20 (2
photos), 21 (center and right), 26, 32, 36, 38, 54 (bottom),
56, 60, 61, 65, 66 (bottom), 70 (top left, bottom left and
right), 71 (top and center left and right), 72 (2 photos), 73
(2 photos), 74 (right), 75 (2 photos), 77 (left), 80 (2
photos), 81 (2 photos), 82, 83, 90 (right), 92 (left), 93, 94,
96, 99, 100, 102 (2 photos), 107 (3 photos), 109, 110, 113
(top left)
SuperStock International, Inc.: 63 (left), 68; © **Kurt**
Scholz, 54 (top), 92 (right)
UPI/Bettmann Newsphotos: 48, 50
Valan: © **Wouterloot-Gregoire,** 22 (top); © **Jeff Foote,** 22
(bottom left); © **Paul L. Janosi,** 22 (bottom right); © **Jean-**
Marie Jro, 29
Len W. Meents: Maps on 67, 75
Courtesy Flag Research Center, Winchester,
Massachusetts 01890: Flag on back cover
Cover: Grasslands in the Cuchilla Grande
Cover Inset: Punta del Este
Cover Inset: Gaucho and cattle

On the Playa Brava at Punta del Este, a whimsical
concrete sculpture of giant toes looms over sunbathers.

TABLE OF CONTENTS

Gently rolling grasslands and hills cover a major part of Uruguay.

Chapter 1

THE EASTERN REPUBLIC
OF URUGUAY

The Republic of Uruguay is the smallest independent Latin-American country in South America. It is on the east coast facing the South Atlantic Ocean, wedged between the two largest countries of the continent. On its northern border is Brazil, and to the west and south, Argentina.

Two rivers separate Uruguay from Argentina—the Uruguay River in the west and the large estuary of the Río de la Plata in the south. (An estuary is the lower end of a river.) The country's location on the east bank of the Uruguay River is the reason for its official title of *La República Oriental del Uruguay*, "The Eastern Republic of Uruguay." The name *Uruguay* is thought to have its origin in the language of the Indians who first inhabited the region, and one possible meaning is "the river of shellfish."

Uruguay is quite unlike any other country in South America. It has no mountains or volcanoes like those of the Andean countries, no Amazon rain forests, jungles, or swamps, no large lakes, and no deserts. It is a country of grasslands and small hills and a long coastal region of attractive bays and beaches.

When the Spaniards arrived early in the sixteenth century, they found only scattered tribes of Indians living in the grasslands. The

The beach at Maldonado, a suburb of Punta del Este

explorers found little to interest them in the region. In particular, there were no rich mineral resources such as those found in Peru and Bolivia. But early in the seventeenth century some cattle were successfully introduced into the colony, and in time the herds became the basis of the country's economy. Uruguay became an independent state early in the nineteenth century, despite attempts by Brazil and Argentina to annex the territory. Since then the republic has experienced periods of instability and chaos—and of peace and prosperity. It has known considerable economic hardship in recent years, yet it remains one of the most friendly countries in South America. Despite the small size of the country, it is a regional leader in economic development and political democracy.

Chapter 2

THE LAND

Covering a territory of 68,037 square miles (176,215 square kilometers), Uruguay can be compared in size to the state of North Dakota. To put the tiny country in perspective with its great neighbors in South America, it is just 1/45 the size of Brazil and 1/15 the size of Argentina. The population is also small. While 150 million people live in Brazil and 32 million in Argentina, the people of Uruguay number just over 3 million. Most of them live in the coastal region and in towns along the Uruguay River. By far the greatest concentration of people is in Montevideo, the capital, which is situated on the north bank of the Río de la Plata estuary.

GRASSLANDS AND HILLS

In its location as a small state between its larger neighbors, Uruguay has features of both countries. It is the meeting point of the warm highlands that extend south from Brazil and the immense, flat Argentine grasslands or plains called pampa. Geologically the northern hills of granite are much older than the pampa.

Minas, a city in the Cuchilla Grande

Within the boundaries of Uruguay there are two main ranges of hills, the Cuchilla de Haedo and the Cuchilla Grande, and they cover much of the north and east of the country. In the southeast the Cuchilla Grande descends toward the coast. The name *cuchilla* comes from the occasional sharp spears of weathered granite ridges that break the skyline. Mostly the hills are gently rounded slopes, interspersed with low plateaus and broad valleys. Some, watered by small streams or brooks, known locally as *arroyos*, are covered with forest and dense vegetation. All the hills are of low altitude, with the highest peak in the country, Mirador Nacional in the southern Cuchilla Grande, only 1,644 feet (501 meters).

A first impression of the grasslands of Uruguay is of an endless landscape stretching to the horizon. The tall prairie grass, similar to that of the Argentine pampa, grows on potash-rich soil and provides good pasture on which sheep and cattle thrive. Over the centuries since the cattle were introduced, the character of the

The wide, leafy branches of the ombú tree provide shade for gauchos and animals.

land has changed somewhat. Originally more of the country was covered with prairie grass and the land was wild and untamed. Then with the creation of large *estancias*, "estates," and later the construction of roads, it became necessary to fence off the grasslands against straying cattle. Now there are fewer trees—but still more than grow on the Argentine pampa—to provide shelter for the cattle from the midday sun.

There are no large towns in the central and northern regions of Uruguay. The largest town is Rivera on the frontier with Brazil, with a population of about fifty-five thousand people. A typical small town has a central plaza, surrounded by low, gray buildings, a few shops supplying essential goods, and perhaps a church and a hotel. Roads leading away from the plaza are lined with one-story buildings and homes, some with small, colorful gardens. Bella Unión and Artigas are two of the most northerly towns, and Tacuarembó, farther south in the foothills of the

Laguna del Diario, one of the many lagoons near the coast

Cuchilla de Haedo, is a small cattle-market town. To the east of the Cuchilla Grande is Treinta y Tres, a town of only about twenty-five thousand people situated close to the Quebrada de los Cuervos, a hilly, rocky region with small streams that has been designated as a national park.

THE COAST

In the north close to the Brazilian border, between the Atlantic and the mainland, an extensive series of lagoons is isolated from the ocean by a wide sandy bar. The main international road between Chuy in Uruguay and Pelotas, Brazil, has been built along the natural barrier, behind which is the principal lagoon, named Laguna Merín from its old Indian name meaning "small."

Numerous rivers empty into Laguna Merín and the land, particularly at its southern end, is low-lying and swampy, making

Lighthouse at La Paloma on the South Atlantic Ocean

it one of the prime wetlands of the region. Here it is possible to see a quarter of a million ducks in an afternoon and to find migrant birds resting on their way north and south. From Laguna Merín the coastline extends in a southwesterly direction until Punta del Este, which marks the change between the open Atlantic and the broad estuary of the Río de la Plata. The coastline, with long sandy beaches broken occasionally by rocky promontories, is backed by a wide strip of level land. Immediately behind the coast, this strip is sparsely populated and varied with many miles of sand dunes, some brackish lagoons, and small streams. Plantations of pine trees brought from Europe have helped control the shifting sand dunes, permitting limited agriculture and, in places such as La Paloma, giving shelter for commercial camping sites and holiday chalets. Behind this sandy coastal strip, the towns of Castillos, Rocha, and San Carlos stand on only marginally higher ground.

From Punta del Este, the coastline turns westward to
Montevideo with Punta Ballena yielding a panoramic view of the
Río de la Plata estuary and more rocky headlands and sandy
beaches. To the west from Montevideo, the coast begins to turn
north and inland, passing Colonia del Sacramento (usually called
simply Colonia) with its historic lighthouse used by countless
navigators setting course for the entrance to the Uruguay River.

RIVERS

There are no large rivers entirely within the borders of
Uruguay. The Uruguay River has its source in the state of Santa
Catarina in southern Brazil, where it is known as the Río de las
Pelotas. It flows westward, forming the boundary between Brazil
and Argentina, and then south, marking the boundary between
Argentina and Uruguay. At *Fray Bentos*, "Brother Bentos," the
Uruguay River becomes a broad channel, as wide as 9 miles (14
kilometers) in places, and then joins the Paraná River of
Argentina in the Río de La Plata estuary. The Uruguay has an
estimated length of 1,000 miles (1,600 kilometers) and the Paraná,
of 2,400 miles (3,862 kilometers), and they are part of the great
Paraná and la Plata river systems of South America.

In the 1970s there was a dispute between Argentina and
Uruguay over the ownership of two small, low islands rising a
few feet above the level of the mouth of the river. Now, it has
been agreed that the larger, Martín García, is Argentine and the
other, Dominguez, is Uruguayan.

Navigation upriver on the Uruguay has always been possible
beyond Fray Bentos to Paysandú. It is navigable for oceangoing

The Uruguay River

ships as far as Paysandú and for smaller river steamers farther upstream to Salto. Paysandú and Salto are the two largest towns in Uruguay outside Montevideo. An international bridge connects Paysandú with Colón in Argentina. Continuing upriver from Paysandú, the course is even, between palm savanna grasslands and narrow, densely wooded areas with arroyos that drain into the main stream. Beside one of these arroyos at Guaviyú, hot springs bubble from the ground as a sign of deep subterranean activity. The warm water has been captured and fed into large pools where people can bathe for relaxation and therapeutic benefit.

Not far upstream from Guaviyú, the Uruguay River is broken by seething rapids, such as *El Hervidero,* "where it boils," with rocky banks on either side. The character of the river changes with more rapids and two substantial towns—Concordia on the Argentine side and *Salto,* meaning "jump" or "leap," in Uruguay.

*Uruguay and Argentina share the power generated
from the Salto Grande hydroelectric dam.*

Ferries run between the two towns, but twelve miles (nineteen kilometers) upstream a road crosses the river on the top of the Salto Grande hydroelectric dam. The dam, completed in 1979 as a joint venture with Argentina, is the country's largest, and behind it the river has formed a lake that reaches almost as far as the northern town of Bella Unión. Farther upstream the river becomes the border between Argentina and Brazil, while a tributary, the Cuareim, from the east forms the Uruguayan border with Brazil along with the Yaguarón River and the Laguna Merín.

The Uruguay River has tributaries such as the Arapey, Daymán, and Queguay, but by far the largest tributary and most important river within the country is the Río Negro. Also with a source in the highlands of southern Brazil, some 62 miles (100 kilometers) from the Uruguay border, the Río Negro is 528 miles (850 kilometers) long, and crosses Uruguay in a northeast to southwest direction between the Cuchilla de Haedo and the Cuchilla Grande, before it empties into the Uruguay River amid a dense eucalyptus and pine forest. Close to the confluence of the two rivers is Mercedes, a popular yachting center in the summer season, and the small town of Santo Domingo, the first town to be founded in Uruguay. Tributaries flowing into the Río Negro include the Tacuarembó and the Yi, together with many small streams covering a drainage of about 40 percent of the country. Hydroelectric dams have led to the creation of three artificial lakes along the river. The largest, approximately in the center of the country and about halfway along the course of the river, is Rincón del Bonete, behind the Dr. Gabriel Terra Dam.

Along the coast some large rivers, such as the Cebollatí and Olimar, flow from the Cuchilla Grande into Laguna Merín, and a few, such as the Santa Lucía River and the San José River, run directly into the Río de la Plata estuary.

CLIMATE

Uruguay lies south of the tropics, and has a pleasant, temperate climate all year round. The summer months are December to March with an average temperature in January, the hottest month, of about seventy degrees Fahrenheit (twenty-one degrees Celsius). During the winter months of June to September, the coldest average temperature in July is only around fifty degrees Fahrenheit (ten degrees Celsius). Nights can be cool, but it seldom freezes. Snow is almost unknown, although 1955 was an exceptional year during which parts of the country were covered with snow.

There are no real regional variations, although the interior of the country tends to be one or two degrees hotter than the coastal zone, which benefits from Atlantic breezes. One factor that does affect the weather in both summer and winter is the wind, and changes in wind can be frequent and quite sudden. The north wind that comes from Brazil is tropical, hot and humid, while that from the south, which crosses the pampa of Argentina and is known as *el pampero*, is dry and cold. Occasionally the two winds meet and violent storms occur.

There are no true rainy and dry seasons in Uruguay. The wettest months are April and May, when the rainfall is heaviest, although rains are more frequent in the winter months. Despite its temperate climate, Uruguay is not free from thunderstorms, which are quite common in the summer months; fogs, though they tend not to last all day; floods; and droughts. Droughts can occur at any time of the year, although they are seldom severe and do not affect the whole country at one time.

FLORA

The best-known tree in Uruguay is the ombú, which resembles a small oak. It grows in country places and its spreading, leafy branches provide good shelter for horsemen and animals. Although ombú wood is soft and useless for building or fuel, the tree, which can survive in even the driest places, has become part of the national heritage. Here and there small woods of imported eucalyptus and pines are scattered across the grasslands, and trees—among them acacia, willows, the leguminous mimosas, and other native species—line the banks of the small rivers. Valued for their wood are the *algarrobo*, "carob tree," and particularly the quebracho, whose wood and bark are used in tanning and dyeing. In the south, close to the coastal region, the

Cattle grazing on palm savanna grassland (left) and tall fluffy plumes of the pampas grass (right)

land is dotted with tall yatay palms, which grow in the low-lying swampy savannas bordering some of the rivers.

In the spring and early summer the grasslands and their often unkempt borders are filled with colorful flowers—verbenas, morning glories, and large purple-headed thistles that turn a rich gold as they dry late in the year. Tall pampas grass with fluffy plumes grows in some humid, sandy places. And there on warm, sunlit days the insect world comes alive with brilliant butterflies and noisy crickets.

BIRDS

After three centuries of extensive cattle raising and despite its gentle rural aspect, the land of Uruguay has undergone considerable changes. Some forest species have disappeared, perhaps forever. The introduction of grasses and trees, the clearing of native forest, and the fencing and drainage have left a

The sizes of birds range from the tiny oven bird (left) to the large, flightless rhea.

new landscape. Alongside a road bordered on either side with grasslands, the telephone wires from village to village are strung on graying wood posts that have become home to the *hornero*, "oven bird." These tiny, brown birds with a lighter, creamy breast build solid, sometimes massive mud nests resembling domed clay ovens set on the wooden crossbars. In some localities almost every post carries a nest and those discarded by the oven birds may later be taken up by other birds including cowbirds, wrens, swallows, and small parrots.

The open grasslands are home to the rhea, a large flightless running bird resembling, but not related to, the ostrich of Africa. Rheas are good swimmers and feed on leaves, roots, and insects, especially grasshoppers. Another, though smaller, bird of the grassland is the red-legged seriema, which keeps mostly to the ground, feeding on small lizards and mammals. The place of the partridge in these grasslands and pastures has been taken by its South American equivalent, the tinamou, which nests on the open

The red-legged seriema (left), the southern lapwing (center), and the burrowing owl

ground, laying eggs with a distinctive, shiny enamellike surface.

The national bird of Uruguay—the *tero* or southern lapwing—is also from the grasslands. It is well known to the country people for its aggressive nature and courage. These lapwings, just over a foot (.3 meter) long, have wings armed with tiny spurs and are frequently seen in pairs. Their nest and young are concealed in the rough grass; to drive off predators the parents utter shrill cries and beat their wings vigorously. Another well-liked bird of these open spaces is a tiny burrowing owl. Seen in the daytime, these owls stand silently, staring from posts or mounds where they perch. Their flight is quick and they move about in pairs, apparently unconcerned about passing country people.

Herons are abundant in the swampy places and beside riverbanks along with kingfishers. Also to be found here are *jacanas,* "lily trotters," which, as their name suggests, possess remarkable feet that allow them to walk with ease across floating vegetation.

Sea lions (above) live in colonies on the island of Isla de Lobos. The capybara (below) is a semiaquatic rodent and the armadillo (below right), which is a nocturnal mammal, is covered with protective bony plates.

FAUNA

Of the surviving mammals there are skunks, small wildcats, foxes, and many small rodents, armadillos, and a few antlered pampas deer. Some groups of these deer are now protected by thoughtful ranch owners. The small rodents are the food for birds of prey. European hares were introduced in the last century and have spread widely. Another familiar animal is the common opossum, very much like the opossum of North America. But less well known are the smaller, reddish opossum that follow the riverbanks and coastal wetlands southward.

The wooded arroyos of the rivers and secluded parts of the Uruguay and Negro rivers are also home to otters and capybara, large semiaquatic rodents that can weigh up to 160 pounds (72.5 kilograms).

A few miles from the coast near Punta del Este the tiny, rocky island of Isla de Lobos is home to large colonies of the common sea lion and the southern fur seal. Both species are valuable economically and have become a great tourist attraction. Seals, and also penguins, are occasionally seen on the mainland coast north of Punta del Este.

Among the more dangerous animals are the snakes. Rattlesnakes are encountered in the stony regions and other pit vipers, known as *crucera* from the markings on their heads, are widespread and extremely venomous.

FISH

The river fish of Uruguay are numerous and of many different kinds. This variety is one of the features of the great river systems

Cleaning fish

of South America because their waters have been closely interlinked for tens of millions of years. Representative of three major groups of fish are dorado, a fine game fish; tiny topminnows, which give birth to live young; and numerous catfish, some of which reach enormous size—one known as a zungaro may exceed one hundred pounds (forty-five kilograms). There is also excellent ocean fishing for sharks, skate, and black corvina.

NATURAL RESOURCES

Uruguay is unfortunate in that, almost alone among South American countries, it has no large mineral resources. Development of some of the small deposits of minerals that do exist, among them iron ore, gold, and copper, has not been considered economical up to now and the limited attempts at oil exploration have not been successful. A greater value is placed on the known deposits of marble, granite, and particularly limestone, which is used in the production of cement. In the north of the country some semiprecious stones, such as agate, are so plentiful that they are found on the surface of the ground.

In its many rivers Uruguay has a good resource of hydroelectricity. Four plants have been constructed with enough output so that some energy can be exported.

Historically and traditionally the country's main resource has been its rich soil and pastures. The prairie grass of Uruguay is considered to be superior to that of Argentina, and most available land has been turned over to cattle and sheep. At present only a very small percentage of land is used for agriculture, but the quality of soil is ideal for crops and it is estimated that 50 percent of Uruguay's soil is arable.

A major, but hardly touched, resource is the fishing grounds off the coast, said to be some of the largest and richest in the world. The coastline also provides a different form of resource, with beautiful beaches and scenery combined with a temperate climate that are ideal for tourism.

POTENTIAL

After a promising start late in the nineteenth and early twentieth centuries, Uruguay's recent history has been marred by internal political and economic problems. The country has relied almost exclusively on its rich pastures, cattle, and sheep as the basis for its development. But there is potential in other resources, notably fish and minerals, and plans are in hand to develop these.

Like many developing countries, Uruguay is burdened with heavy international debts, but is without the problem of overpopulation and geographical difficulties that often hinder progress.

The rich, rolling landscape on which animals graze and plants thrive helps make agriculture the base of Uruguay's economy.

Chapter 3
THE BANDA ORIENTAL

THE CHARRÚA INDIANS

When Europeans first arrived in the land that is now Uruguay, early in the sixteenth century, they found the country inhabited by Indians. There were several groups, like the Chana and the Bohanes, but the largest tribe was the Charrúa. Ancestors of the Charrúa, together with many of the native people of South America, are thought to have arrived on the continent some ten thousand to twenty thousand years ago, making their way from Asia across the Bering Strait toward the end of the Ice Age. It is possible that some of the earliest tribes arrived before the extinction of the very large animals, such as the glyptodon and giant sloth (an early ancestor of the armadillo). In the beginning they survived by hunting and fishing.

As the centuries passed, some tribes settled into communities and became simple farmers; others, including the Charrúa, continued to exist by hunting, fishing, and gathering wild fruits. The pampa were plentiful with various kinds of wildlife. For weapons, the Charrúa used bows and arrows, slings, spears, and *bolas*, weapons used in hunting animals. The Charrúa type of bolas had just one stone attached to a fiber cord that was decorated at the end with a tuft of rhea feathers. They would whirl this device through the air to trap their victim with the cord as the weight spun around its legs or some other part of the body. After the Spaniards arrived, the Indians began to use the more traditional bolas—a y-shaped cord with three stones attached.

The Charrúa also were expert with the arrow and, tipped with a stone head, this weapon is said to have had a range of up to 300 feet (91 meters). Physically the Charrúa are known to have been tall—women averaging 5.4 feet (1.63 meters) and men, 5.5 feet (1.65 meters). They are described as always having a sad expression, but in war they were ferocious opponents. In preparation for a battle they would hide their families in nearby woods and then advance on the enemy in a surprise attack. They fought fearlessly and without mercy, but always spared women and children. It is said that after the battle was won, they skinned the heads of their victims, making ceremonial drinking cups of the skulls.

A typical Charrúa home was made of four poles with the walls and roof made from straw mats. The Charrúa cooked animal meat in pots made of black clay decorated with zigzag lines. They tattooed their faces, using different designs for each tribe. Ear pendants of bone or feathers, copper pieces in the nostrils, and thin lip plugs were additional adornments. For clothing they used deer hides fashioned like aprons and animal furs worn as long cloaks during the winter months.

Spanish explorers noted beautiful canoes fashioned by the Charrúa, which they used for transport and fishing. Built of cedar wood, they were elaborately carved, decorated with crests and tassels of feathers, and rowed with long paddles by forty standing men. Some two hundred years later a traveler noted that the Charrúa had ceased to use canoes. Instead they had become expert

The estuary of the Río de la Plata at Montevideo

horsemen. The horse was introduced by the Spaniards and enabled the Indians to cross the pampa quickly when hunting the rhea and other animals.

DISCOVERY AND SETTLEMENT

The first Europeans to sail toward the coast of Uruguay were searching for a passage from the Atlantic to the Pacific Ocean, and on approaching the wide estuary of the Río de la Plata they might be forgiven for thinking they had found it. In 1516 a group led by the Spanish explorer Juan Díaz de Solís arrived at the great river and landed on the coast near the present-day town of Maldonado. Here Díaz de Solís was killed by the Charrúa. Although probably not the first to enter the river, Díaz de Solís is credited with its discovery. He named it the Santa Maria, and after his death it was known for some years, in his honor, as the Solís River. Some survivors of his expedition heard rumors of a mountainous country upriver where people explored for and mined large

*Sebastian Cabot,
the Italian explorer
who named the river
the Río de la Plata*

amounts of gold and silver. These rumors came to the notice of
Sebastián Cabot, the Italian explorer, who sailed from Spain in
1526.

A recorder on the Cabot expedition wrote when they arrived at
the Río de la Plata estuary: "This is a very powerful river, twenty-
five leagues wide at its mouth. We were to encounter many
difficulties and dangers in the river; it is full of shoals . . . it is
subject to violent storms." Nevertheless, after making inquiries of
the local Indians, Cabot decided to proceed up the Paraná River,
through present-day Argentina, and into Paraguay in his search
for riches. He made no attempt to explore the land to the east of
the Uruguay River, known then as the *Banda Oriental*, or "east
bank," as opposed to the "west bank," which today is Argentina.
Upriver, his expedition met with limited success but he did return
with some silver, and so the name of the river was changed to the
Río de la Plata, "River of Silver," or Plate River.

The next large expedition to the Río de la Plata region was led
by Pedro de Mendoza in 1535. On board he carried a hundred

horses, pigs, and horned cattle. The aim of the expedition was to settle, rather than explore, and Mendoza will be remembered as the man who founded Buenos Aires on the banks of the Río de la Plata. He too made no effort to cross into the Banda Oriental, and it was not until 1603 that Hernando Arias (usually known as Hernandarias), the first locally born governor of the Río de la Plata region, made the inspired decision to send cattle there. From his governmental headquarters in Asunción, Paraguay, he sent one hundred head of cattle and one hundred horses down the river into the Banda Oriental.

The good pastureland meant that soon the cattle were multiplying and it was not long before *gauchos*, "cowboys," were arriving from the west bank to kill the cattle for their hides. Gauchos were nomadic horsemen who spent their lives out on the open pampa rearing and herding cattle. They were followed by merchants prepared to settle, and a trade in hides developed. This marked the beginning of real Spanish interest in the colony.

About this time, Franciscan and Jesuit missionaries also arrived, as the Spanish crown placed great importance on the need to convert the native populations of the newly acquired colonies to Christianity. It was difficult and dangerous work but the missionaries met with some success among groups of less hostile Indians.

In 1680 the Portuguese, who had taken over much of present-day Brazil, pushed south and founded a settlement at Colonia, the nearest point on the north side of Río de la Plata opposite Buenos Aires. This action provoked a conflict between Portugal and Spain that was to last for almost one hundred years.

In colonial times Spain forbade her territories to trade independently with other nations, even though Spain was unable

Colonia, the oldest settlement in the country

to supply all the goods that the colonies needed. So the region became an open market for smugglers and illegal traders, with the Portuguese in Colonia controlling not only the Río de la Plata but the routes upriver to other Spanish colonies. This was an intolerable state of affairs for the Spanish crown, and there were many invasions and many attempts by treaty to resolve the matter. In one, signed in Madrid in 1750, it was agreed that Spain should have Colonia in return for a vast area of land occupied by the Jesuit missions close to the northern border with Brazil. The matter did not end there however; Colonia changed hands again, and the conflict was only brought to a close in 1776 when the governor of Buenos Aires marched on Colonia and destroyed the city. The Portuguese, however, kept the land awarded them in the 1750 treaty.

The Spaniards began their occupation of the Banda Oriental when they founded the city of Montevideo in 1726. To administer the conquered lands in the New World, the Spanish crown divided the whole territory into viceroyalties, each headed by a viceroy. In 1776 the Banda Oriental became part of the Viceroyalty of the United Provinces of the Río de la Plata centered in Buenos Aires. During the eighteenth century, cattlemen from Buenos Aires continued to occupy land on the riverbank, gradually spreading into the interior. It became necessary to fix boundaries and in this way great estancias where created. Small trading towns were established on roads connecting the estancias to Montevideo and the coast.

THE BRITISH IN MALDONADO

Early in the nineteenth century the British sent military and naval expeditions to the Río de la Plata region. There were commercial considerations. In 1778, in response to increasing resentment among the *criollo* (people of Spanish parentage born in the colonies) merchants against restriction of trade, the Spanish crown passed legislation permitting free trade between the colonies and the rest of the world. The result was a commercial boom, not only in Europe but for some of the colonies. The traders in the Río de la Plata region did particularly well: in five years the export of hides through Buenos Aires rose from 150,000 a year to about 1.4 million.

But the British government also had another interest: it hoped to encourage the overthrow of Spanish authority in the New World. The two countries had long been rivals in their quest for supremacy in Europe and in the acquisition of new colonies. In Europe Spanish power was declining, and already in some colonies anti-Spanish protests and revolts had occurred—with strong calls for independence. In 1806 the British captured Buenos

Aires, but two months later the criollos took it back. They had no more desire to be controlled by the British than by the Spanish crown. The British retreated to Maldonado on the bank of the Río de la Plata to await reinforcements from England. They enjoyed the pleasures of the coast and were treated well by the locals who supplied them with food. When reinforcements eventually arrived, they were considered insufficient for the recapture of Buenos Aires and the British contingent, under the command of General Samuel Auchmuty, attacked the city of Montevideo instead. A fierce battle ensued, with many lives lost, but the British emerged victorious.

Off the coast and anchored in the Río de la Plata were many small boats with merchants from Britain who, having heard of the British capture of Buenos Aires, set sail with their merchandise. They did not know that the city had been retaken by the criollos. So when they discovered that they could not sell their goods in Buenos Aires, they had no option but to do business with the people of the Banda Oriental. Locals and foreigners got on well together. The inhabitants of Montevideo had never known such an abundance of fine European manufactured goods, including silk stockings, furniture, and brandy, and they learned something of the political affairs of Europe. The British, hoping to encourage the spread of democratic ideas and at the same time criticize Spain's arbitrary rule and the growing threat of Napoleon in Europe, arranged for a weekly newspaper called the *Southern Star* to be printed in English and Spanish. In it, these issues were openly discussed. Eventually the British were forced to leave Montevideo and the Río de la Plata region when a final expedition to take Buenos Aires failed, but their brief stay had furthered the desire for change among many people in Banda Oriental.

JOSÉ GERVASIO ARTIGAS

News that Napoleon had deposed Ferdinand VII and put his brother Joseph on the Spanish throne hastened events in the colonies. In 1810 the Spanish viceroy in Buenos Aires was deposed and Argentina declared its independence in 1816. It might have been supposed that independence in the Banda Oriental would have been a mere formality then, but it was not achieved until twelve years later.

The hero of the Uruguayan struggle was José Gervasio Artigas. His Spanish grandfather had arrived in Buenos Aires in 1716 and after ten years he volunteered to take his family to help in the founding of Montevideo. He and his son, José's father, were both distinguished military horsemen. The young José was destined for the church, but after some years of study he renounced the religious life and was sent by his father to the family estancia. Far from being a punishment, Artigas enjoyed the open-air life among the gauchos and cattle. He became a soldier for a time and was involved in creating new communities for settlers along the border with Brazil. From time to time he had to defend these new settlements against Portuguese incursions, leading a strangely assorted, but loyal, army which included local Indians and gauchos. Artigas acquired a reputation as a leader and a fighter.

The battle for supremacy over the Banda Oriental was fought between the military junta who had replaced the Spaniards in Buenos Aires, the Spanish representative still in power in Montevideo, and the Portuguese who were anxious to claim the territory for Brazil. At times, the *Orientales*, as the people of the Banda were known, fought between themselves as well as against the criollos of Argentina who wanted to annex the territory.

*An equestrian statue of
José Gervasio Artigas,
the general who led
the fight for independence
against Brazil and Portugal*

At the beginning of the fighting, Artigas, now recognized as the national leader, gave his support to the Buenos Aires junta against the Spanish governor in Montevideo. But when the governor called on the Portuguese and Brazilians for assistance, the junta withdrew, leaving Artigas without allies. Disillusioned by the junta's withdrawal and recognizing that he could not take on the combined forces of the Portuguese and Spanish, Artigas decided to leave the Banda. To his surprise thousands of his countrymen joined him, in what has become known as the "Exodus." Men, women, and children, gauchos and Indians, cattle and ox carts— all made up the extraordinary band of exiles who made the long trek across the country and the Uruguay River into Argentina. There they remained for some fourteen months, conducting a campaign of guerrilla tactics and harassment against the armies in the Banda Oriental. They lived on beef and water, under whatever shelter they could find—trees, their ox carts, or some makeshift hut—and although a few had muskets and swords, the majority fought only with their gaucho knives and bolas. The event marked the birth of a real sense of national identity among the Orientales.

Artigas returned to the Banda Oriental in 1813 to support the Buenos Aires junta once more against the Spanish in Montevideo. In return for his cooperation he sought the junta's agreement in securing independent status for the Banda Oriental. When the junta failed to agree, Artigas again withdrew his support. Once more he sought refuge close to the Uruguay River, though this time in the east bank. From there he was able to make contact with several provinces in Argentina, which for one reason or another also refused to accept the authority of the Buenos Aires junta. It was part of his plan, even his dream, to create a federation of provinces of the Río de la Plata region.

Eventually Montevideo fell to the junta, who in turn were expelled from the city by the Orientales. But Artigas remained with his army of gauchos and Indians in the interior. He tried to keep his federation together, but in the face of another invasion from Brazil and a three-year-long battle against its stronger forces, he was forced into exile in Paraguay—an exile from which he never returned.

Brazil occupied the Banda Oriental for five years. Meanwhile exiles in Argentina, who had fought with Artigas, plotted the overthrow of the invaders and finally, in April 1825, thirty-three

Juan Antonio Lavalleja was the leader of the "Immortal Thirty-Three."

men known as the "Immortal Thirty-Three," led by Juan Antonio Lavalleja, crossed the Uruguay River in rowboats. Their countrymen eagerly awaited them. Backed by the Argentine government, which was anxious to expel the Portuguese, they headed for Montevideo. Once again war was waged between the two nations.

When the Portuguese blocked the Río de la Plata, the British, who for some time had been concerned about their trade in the region, decided to intervene. Believing that, in any case, it would be beneficial to have a buffer state between the two great warring South American republics, the British government exerted all its influence to bring about a peaceful solution. Independence of the Banda Oriental was finally achieved in 1828, with the creation of the República Oriental del Uruguay.

Chapter 4

A NEW NATION

COLORADOS AND BLANCOS: "REDS" AND "WHITES"

Independence did not bring peace to the new republic and for much of the nineteenth century Uruguay was in a state of turmoil. Early on the two main contenders for power were generals who had fought in the wars of independence—José Fructuoso Rivera who emerged as the country's first president, and Manuel Oribe who succeeded him. Such men were known as *caudillos,* and in several South American countries caudillos dominated the political scene in the nineteenth century. They built up a cult of leadership based on their personal popularity and their willingness to use violence in the pursuit of power.

The people of Uruguay were divided in their support. Followers of Rivera became known as the *Colorados,* "Reds," because his lancers carried red pennants on their spearheads. Oribe, leader of the *Blancos,* "Whites," rode a white horse and his men had white pennants. The colors and causes of the rival factions are historically significant because they were the basis for the formation of Uruguay's two main political parties. Today these are still known as the Colorados and the Blancos, although the Blancos have now officially become the National party, *Partido Nacional.*

General José Fructuoso Rivera (left) was defeated by General Juan Manuel de Rosas (right).

Each side looked to neighboring countries for support, and some European nations became involved when their interests were at stake. In 1838 Rivera, backed by the French, deposed Oribe as president and installed himself for a second term, and so began a period of civil war that lasted until 1851. The Blancos drew their support from the church, and from the countryside where most of the land was owned by a few wealthy families who had established their estates during the colonial period. The Colorados controlled Montevideo and other urban centers.

Oribe sought help from the infamous Argentine dictator, Juan Manuel de Rosas, and for nine years Montevideo was besieged by Argentine forces. French and Italian soldiers helped in the defense of the city, and the British and French navies blockaded Argentine ports. The war ended only when Rosas himself was deposed and the siege of Montevideo was lifted. But the tiny war-torn country was to experience yet more fighting. The Colorados were now in control under General Venancio Flores, the new president. On two occasions he was obliged to seek Brazilian assistance to keep him in power. In return Uruguay was forced into the devastating War of the Triple Alliance, fighting alongside Brazil and Argentina against the dictator Francisco Solano López of Paraguay. By the end of the war in 1870 both Flores and his main Blanco opponent had been assassinated.

The Colorados had political control throughout the remaining years of the nineteenth century, though their rule was often subject to revolts and assassinations by opposing Blancos, who were demanding a greater share in government. Toward the end of the century, following a Blanco uprising and the assassination of a Colorado president, tension between the two factions erupted. By 1904 the country was again in the throes of a civil war.

SETTLERS AND DEVELOPMENT

So much fighting in the first four decades of the republic took its toll, particularly in the interior where the estates and cattle herds were neglected. Very little land was cultivated. Outside the towns there were no roads or bridges; rivers had to be crossed on horseback. On the other hand, Montevideo, while at the center of some of the fiercest battles, was still an important commercial port. Small numbers of European immigrants, recognizing the potential of the tiny republic, began to settle there, even during the worst years of fighting.

Many thousands more immigrants arrived in the last quarter of the century, as the country settled into a period of relative peace. They introduced agriculture to the coastal zone, developed retail trades such as textiles and leather goods, and were involved in shipping and other commercial activities. Pedigreed sheep and

This engraving shows tall sailing ships in the port of Montevideo in the 1800s.

cattle were imported, greatly improving the quality of beef and wool, which were in demand for the export market. The first textile mill was established in the 1880s. Small local industries developed and gradually foreign companies gained sufficient confidence to invest in public works and other services in the republic. Montevideo had the first electric plant in South America, installed in 1886, and the British built a gasworks. The telephone was first tried in the capital in 1878, and by the 1890s, Montevideo had more telephones per person than any other city in South America.

One of the most important investments was a railway system, which opened up the country and facilitated the transport of goods between the interior and the coast. The port of Montevideo also was improved and enlarged, taking advantage of the deeper waters on the north side of the Río de la Plata. Before the turn of the century ships had to discharge their cargo on barges in the harbor, but by 1908, once the port was modernized, large oceangoing vessels could dock for loading and unloading.

A CUP
THAT CHEERS
and gratefully warms the
system after exposure to
cold or dampness is
made with hot water and
a little of the genuine

Liebig
COMPANY'S
Extract of Beef

*An 1890s advertisement for extract
of beef produced by the London-based
Liebig's Extract of Meat Company.*

Of particular note was the development of the meat extract
business, based in the small port of Fray Bentos on the Uruguay
River. The business was founded by a German, G. C. Giebert,
using a process first devised by another German, Justus Liebig.
Liebig, director of the Royal Pharmacy at Munich, began
experiments to produce a concentrated extract of meat that could
be used to help the sick. His experiments were successful, but the
price of cattle in Europe was too high for the product to be
profitable commercially. Giebert arrived in Uruguay looking for
work and, knowing of Liebig's experiments, realized the
possibilities in a land where cattle were cheap—indeed unwanted
carcasses were left lying on the ground. In the early 1860s, he
built his first factory and dispatched his first exports. In 1866 the
Liebig's Extract of Meat Company was formed in London. From
the beginning it was a great success. By 1875 the production of the
extract in Uruguay reached 1 million pounds (453,600 kilograms)
a year, and by 1890, 5 million pounds (2.3 million kilograms),
with some 3 million cattle being processed.

However, by 1890, the meat extract had already become a by-product of an even more profitable business. Due to the development of canning techniques, the factory at Fray Bentos was able to produce canned corned beef, which proved to be an important export until well after World War II.

In the years before and after Uruguay's independence, very little consideration had been given to the social and educational needs of the people. In the 1870s the cause of educational reform was taken up by a concerned young man, José Pedro Varela, who had the sympathetic ear of the dictator Colonel Lorenzo Latorre. Varela proposed that, as in the United States, everyone should be entitled to free primary education, which he believed was the first stepping-stone to a civilized, democratically run country. His plan met considerable opposition from the university professors representing the educational establishment, and from the church who viewed it as too liberal. Nonetheless it became law in 1877. There was a certain irony in the passage of the Varela law because it was achieved during the rule of a military dictatorship, and it might have proved too liberal and progressive for even a democratic congress at that time. It was Colonel Latorre who made sure that the bill was passed. Although a dictator, he made it clear that he wanted democracy for the country, and he agreed with Varela that this meant first educating the people. From then until his untimely death at the age of thirty-four, José Pedro Varela worked ceaselessly to put his plans into operation.

THE WELFARE STATE

The civil war of 1904 lasted eight months and occurred during the first year of the presidency of Uruguay's most renowned politician, the Colorado leader José Batlle y Ordóñez. He crushed the Blanco rebellion effectively and decisively, but not without recognizing the reason behind the struggle. The Colorados or the military had been in power continuously since independence, much to the frustration of the Blancos who felt they should be represented in government. The war ended with an agreement between the two parties that heralded a long period of internal peace and orderly government in Uruguay.

José Batlle y Ordóñez was a reformer and an educated man who not only transformed Uruguay from a war-torn country to a stable, prosperous nation, but was largely responsible for the creation of the first "welfare state" in South America.

As a young man he was a political journalist. He founded his own newspaper, *El Día*, at the age of thirty. Batlle y Ordóñez used the paper as a forum for discussing the nation's problems; he became leader of the Colorados, and was twice president of the republic. Between his presidencies, he spent time in Europe studying the ways of government, particularly in Switzerland, and developing his social ideas. He was very conscious of the growing gap between the rich and poor in Uruguay, and when he returned for his second term as president, he introduced sweeping reforms that affected the political, social, and economic life of the nation. The list of proposed reforms was long and very advanced for the time. It included labor legislation allowing for an eight-hour working day, one day off in every five worked, the right to strike, accident insurance, and old-age pensions. In the economic field, he believed the state should own the country's major industries, including power, communication, insurance, and alcohol and tobacco, and he advocated the building of more railways. These reforms infuriated the conservatives and also the Catholic church, who saw its power seriously eroded. The church lost control of education, and religious teaching in schools was no longer obligatory; women were given the right to divorce, and people did not have to marry in church. By 1919 the functions of the church and the state had been separated completely.

Under Batlle y Ordóñez, constitutional reform also became a big issue. He argued that power should not be vested in a president, as he believed this led to dictatorship. Instead he advocated that the office of president should be banned and that an Executive Council, a form of committee, should govern the country. This was a truly radical proposal that even many of his supporters were unable to accept. The result, which had the agreement of the Colorado and Blanco parties, was a new constitution that came into effect in 1919 after he had left office. It was essentially a compromise with power shared between a president and a National Council of Administration. The Council was made up of nine members elected by the people, six from the majority party and three from the minority party. This arrangement did not last, however, and the constitution has been changed many times since then. Nonetheless the reforms introduced by Batlle y Ordóñez set the country on the path to democratic government and for most of the twentieth century Uruguay has enjoyed the reputation of being one of the most democratic countries in Latin America.

TWO WORLD WARS

During World War I, Uruguay enjoyed an economic boom based on the export of meat and wool. The standard of living was good. Relations with the United States became closer and, after the war, North American investors helped to finance roads and industries. The Colorados continued in power throughout the 1920s and 1930s, but could do little to prevent a decline in the Uruguayan economy, particularly when the New York Stock Market crashed in 1929 at the time of a worldwide economic depression.

The economy picked up again during World War II, when meat and wool were again in demand. Small manufacturing industries developed to supply goods that could no longer be imported. There was less unemployment and working conditions improved.

At the beginning of World War II, Uruguay remained neutral, supporting neither the British, the United States, and their allies on the one hand nor the Germans and their allies on the other. The Blancos, still the party in opposition, had leanings toward the Germans, and fought to keep North American naval bases off Uruguayan territory. Neighboring Argentina supported the Germans and applied pressure on Uruguay to do the same. But Uruguay, though it did not actively take part in the conflict, declared war on Germany and its allies in 1945 at the end of the war.

However, Uruguay will be remembered for its part in an incident that happened much earlier in the war.

In 1939, three British cruisers, the *Exeter*, *Ajax*, and *Achilles*, were patrolling the waters close to the Río de la Plata to protect ships carrying vital cargoes from South America to Europe. A German ship, the *Graf Spee*, was sighted by the British vessels and they attacked the Germans. The *Graf Spee* was hit. In accordance with the rules of war, the *Graf Spee* was entitled to remain in port for just four days for repairs before putting out to sea once again. Had the Uruguay authorities been sympathetic to the Germans, they would have given the *Graf Spee* more time, but they made

The German ship, Graf Spee, *burning off the coast of Montevideo*

certain the ship left Montevideo in the specified four days. When the *Graf Spee* steamed out of the Río de la Plata, the British cruisers were waiting. The German captain had little choice but to order his crew to abandon ship. The *Graf Spee* was scuttled, and her hulk sank in the Río de la Plata. For many years it was possible to see the control tower sticking out of the water, but the hull has now been dismantled. The German crew made their way to Argentina where they were welcomed as heroes.

TROUBLED TIMES AND TERRORISTS

Uruguay's relationship with Argentina, bad during the war, became considerably worse in the ten years following. General Juan Perón was president of Argentina and many of his enemies were granted asylum in Uruguay, from where they made continual attacks against the Perón regime using Uruguayan

Uruguay sheltered many enemies of the president of Argentina, Juan Perón. Because of this, Perón forbade Argentines to vacation in Uruguay and devastated Uruguay's economy.

newspapers and radio for anti-Perón propaganda. Perón retaliated by forbidding Argentines to take their holidays in Uruguay, which had a devastating effect on the Uruguayan tourist trade. The country's economy was already suffering because exports of meat and wool dropped after the war. There was high inflation and not enough money to support the demands of the welfare state. The people were dissatisfied and there were outbreaks of violence and riots.

Between 1951 and 1966, there was no president and the country was ruled by a collective leadership. In the general elections of 1958, the Blancos, or National party, won the majority of votes for the first time in ninety-three years. During the 1960s, when the Blancos were again elected, and in the 1970s, the deteriorating situation led to social upheaval, an economic crisis, and terrorism.

The Movement of National Liberation, a terrorist group more

Juan Bordaberry, president of the Colorado party, became president in 1972. He did crush the Tupamaros, but he is remembered for his repressive regime.

popularly known as the Tupamaros, emerged. The name *tupamaro* is derived from Tupac-Amaru, the last of the Inca leaders in eighteenth-century Peru. The group was led by Raúl Sendic, a leader of the sugar workers in the north of the country. Influenced by the Cuban revolution of 1959, Sendic believed that the power of the ruling conservative political classes could only be broken by an armed struggle. In the ensuing years, the country suffered from widespread terrorist activities, although some of the Tupamaro's actions had popular appeal. They robbed a series of banks, distributed to the poor food stolen from supermarkets, and on one occasion organized a spectacular jailbreak in which more than one hundred Tupamaros tunneled out through Montevideo's drainage system. Their activities attracted students and some of the professional and middle classes, but the group went too far when they assassinated a United States police adviser and kidnapped a British ambassador in 1971.

The country had had enough. A new Colorado president, Juan Bordaberry, was elected in 1971 and the army stepped in to crush the guerrillas. A year later the Tupamaros were defeated. Then the military took over, insisting on the closure of Congress and its replacement by an appointed Council of State. The Council was composed of civilian and military members, but it was the military that wielded power. Thousands of people were secretly detained, and Sendic himself was sentenced to forty-five years in prison. Trade unions were stopped from demonstrating, left-wing groups and the Communist party were banned, and there was wide press censorship. As the numbers of political prisoners grew—by 1976 thought to be about six thousand—the regime was internationally criticized as one of Latin America's most repressive regimes.

It was a great shock to the people of Uruguay, whose democratic traditions had always been regarded highly among Latin American nations. Despite considerable pressure, the military remained in power until 1985, when it agreed to a return of normal political activity. Elections were held, the Colorados secured a narrow victory, and Dr. Julio María Sanguinetti was installed as president. One of the first actions of his government was to release all political prisoners, including Raúl Sendic, as well as some nine thousand common criminals, and to legalize political and other organizations that had been banned under the military.

In 1986 Sanguinetti introduced his most controversial legislation: an amnesty for all military and police personnel accused of crimes against humanity committed during the military dictatorship. There was furious opposition to this legislation and, in accordance with the terms of the Uruguayan constitution, opponents organized a petition and gathered signatures from 25 percent of the population, thus forcing a

*Uruguayans cheered when Dr. Julio María Sanguinetti (left)
became president and ended years of military rule.*

referendum—a popular vote on the matter. Many families had
been affected by military abuse, but also there was a strong desire
for peace and time to put the country's economy in order. The
referendum supported President Sanguinetti and all parties agreed
to respect the result.

By far the most difficult task facing the new government was
the failing economy, which led to numerous protests and strikes
organized by the unions and other workers. The standard of
living had dropped disastrously: there were food shortages,
widespread malnutrition, inflation, and high unemployment. The
once-high prices commanded by Uruguay's main exports had
been affected by the fall in world prices and attempts to diversify
the economy had not been successful. President Sanguinetti's
government made little headway and in 1989 two twenty-four-
hour strikes brought the country to a standstill. It was significant
that in municipal elections in the same year the country's third

Luis Alberto Lacalle and his wife celebrate the news of victory on presidential election day, November 26, 1989.

political party, the left-wing Frente Amplio, secured a notable victory by winning the office of mayor of Montevideo, the most powerful post in the country after the presidency.

In Uruguay's 1989 national elections the candidate for the National party (Blancos) won by a small majority. The new president was Luis Alberto Lacalle, grandson of Luis Alberto Herrera, the Blanco's greatest leader. To make his government workable, President Lacalle was obliged to form a coalition with other parties, and their first priority was the economy.

GOVERNMENT

There have been many changes since the first constitution of 1830. The government of today is based on the constitution of 1966 when the country voted for a return to presidential government.

The Legislative Palace (above) and the new presidential offices (left), with a statue of José Gervasio Artigas

The president, who is chief of state and commander of the armed forces, is elected for a five-year term. Every citizen over the age of eighteen has the right to vote. The president has a vice-president who is also the president of Congress. The president and vice-president must be over thirty-five years old and citizens of Uruguay. They exercise executive power with an appointed Council of Ministers.

Legislative power lies with the Congress, or General Assembly, which is made up of two houses, the Senate and the Chamber of

Deputies. There are thirty senators and ninety-nine
members of the Chamber of Deputies, all elected for five
years.

A Supreme Court consisting of five members, tribunals, and
local courts is responsible for the administration of justice. The
Supreme Court, whose members must be over forty years of age
and have specified legal experience, appoints all other judges and
law officials.

The constitution also states that 25 percent of the electorate can
force a referendum to reconsider a law passed by Congress.
Uruguay has held thirteen national referendums in its history.
The first, in 1917, resulted in the separation of the Catholic church
and the state. The most recent, in 1989, supported President
Sanguinetti's amnesty for military officers accused of human
rights abuses.

Uruguay has nineteen departments (states), each governed by a
departmental council and a legislative assembly, both of which are
elected by the people.

NATIONAL DEFENSE

Uruguay has an army, navy, and air force. The armed forces are
made up of volunteers, aged between eighteen and forty-five, who
sign up for one or two years of service. In 1990, the total force
numbered 25,200 with 68 percent in the army, 18 percent in the
navy, and 14 percent in the air force. The army comprises
regiments of cavalry, engineers, infantry, artillery, and tanks.
There also are paramilitary forces of about 2,650.

The Last of the Charrúa *monument, depicting native
Americans who once inhabited Uruguay, is in Montevideo.*

Chapter 5

THE PEOPLE

OF URUGUAY

The population of Uruguay—approximately three million—is small in relation to the size of the country. The population is unevenly distributed. More than half live in and around Montevideo, where most of the manufacturing industries are based, and in the agricultural zone along the coast. Most Uruguayans, about 90 percent of the population, are descendants of immigrants who arrived in the nineteenth and twentieth centuries. The remainder are people of mixed races. The mixed races are *mestizos,* who are part Spanish and part Indian, and *mulattos* who are of African and Spanish descent. By the early twentieth century the indigenous Charrúa and other Indians had disappeared and Uruguay is now the only country in South America without an Indian population.

THE LAND OF THE CHARRÚA

There is a monument in a park in central Montevideo called *The Last of the Charrúa.* It is a poignant reminder of the people who once inhabited the Banda Oriental, depicting four members of the tribe gathered around a hearth. A woman holds her baby, and the men, cast in typical dress, wear a brave but saddened expression.

Unlike Indians in the Andes or the tropical lowlands, who could escape to high mountains or vast forests, the Indians of Uruguay's open grasslands had no refuge. Many lived on the coast where the Europeans first landed. From the time the Spaniards and other explorers arrived and settled in the Banda Oriental, the days of the Indian peoples were numbered. There were several reasons for this. Not the least was disease, which killed many of the natives who never before had been exposed to epidemics of smallpox, measles, typhus, plague, yellow fever, and malaria. Other Indians were killed in skirmishes with the Spaniards— sometimes in defense of their land, sometimes when they raided the herds and tried to steal cattle. Still others were taken as slaves by the settlers and forced to work in conditions that led to illness or death. Yet another reason for the decline in the Indian population was integration. Many explorers and settlers who arrived in the colony without wives or families married native women, and, over the years, as the number of mestizos increased, the number of pure Indians decreased.

Some more fortunate Indians were taken in by Jesuit missions and protected from enslavement. The Jesuits, whose aim was to convert as many Indians as possible to Christianity, treated them kindly. There was ample food and the Indians were taught how to grow crops and rear cattle. There were hospitals for the sick, schools where the young could learn to read and write, and for some of the more artistic, training in painting, carving, and music. Women learned to weave and some items of cloth and hide were traded for goods needed in the missions. The missions were a success but they were greatly resented by the landowners who wanted the Indians to work for them. In time the Spanish government was persuaded that the missions had become too powerful, and the Jesuits were expelled from the territory in 1767. It was a sad day for the Indians, whose inevitable fate was then in the hands of the settlers.

IMMIGRANTS

When Uruguay became a republic in 1830, the population numbered only about seventy thousand. Immigrants began to arrive soon after independence, but because of the unsettled nature of the country their numbers were limited. Among the first arrivals were Italians, French, British, Lebanese, Jewish, and Armenians. Mostly they settled in Montevideo where they set themselves up in small trading concerns, in import and export firms, and in shipping. A greater wave of immigrants arrived in the second half of the nineteenth century, when the country had achieved a degree of peace. Many, however, were tempted to cross into Argentina where prospects were more favorable. Owing partly to the progressive polices of Batlle y Ordóñez, immigrant numbers increased considerably between 1900 and 1930, with an average of fifteen thousand people arriving each year. It has been calculated that between 1836 and 1926 some 648,000 immigrants entered Urugray.

The immigrants brought new ideas and technical knowledge to the new republic. Until their arrival, the economy had been based almost exclusively on cattle and the large estancias, but the new arrivals, particularly those from Mediterranean countries, preferred to cultivate crops. They developed small farms, particularly in the coastal areas, where they could grow vegetables and a variety of fruits well known in Europe. Among some of the more prosperous agricultural communities were the Swiss Colony

The owner of a cheese shop near Nueva Helvicia

and the Waldenese, composed entirely of Italians. The colonies exist today, though in name only, close to the small town of Nueva Helvecia, "New Switzerland," not far from Colonia. Not all their tradition is lost, however, as a few shops sell Swiss cheese and Swiss music boxes, and the Swiss national day on August 1 is still celebrated. The oldest Evangelical church in South America was founded in the nearby village of La Paz.

The British were prominent among the immigrants. Some were involved in the construction of the railroads and gasworks in the nineteenth century, while others brought herds of pedigree cattle and sheep and founded estancias in the interior. Many went to the province of the Río Negro, which is said to have the most fertile land. The town of Young is named after an English cabinetmaker who arrived in the 1820s because he was commissioned to carve doors for the new cathedral. When the job was finished, cabinetmaker Young and his friend Mr. Stirling bought land and settled down. The estancia they founded is still well known today as a breeder of fine cattle and sheep.

Horse-drawn carts are used by the residents of San Javier, founded by people from Russia.

Far from home, but often with neighbors from Scotland or England, the pioneers made life as comfortable as possible, growing most of their foodstuffs on the estancias. Children were educated at home and sometimes a governess was brought from England. Eventually a British school and British hospital were built in Montevideo. One beach is still referred to as Playa de los Ingleses, "English Beach," and British tradition was firmly established with the opening of the Cricket Club.

Many twentieth-century immigrants went to Uruguay as a result of troubles in their own countries. Communities from Central Europe and the Middle East included Poles, Romanians, Soviets, Turks, and Lebanese, as well as thousands of Jewish refugees from Germany. One of the last groups to arrive was Mennonites who fled from Poland at the outbreak of World War II. They founded a farming community at Colonia El Ombú just south of the town of Young. At San Javier, a village on the Uruguay River south of Paysandú, there is a community of Russian descent. Several generations have passed since the first

The naturalist Charles Darwin described the colorful gauchos of Uruguay after his visit in 1832.

families arrived, but the villagers still live in much the same way as the rural people of Eastern Europe. Horse-drawn carts clatter along the dusty streets and fishermen on the river use rowboats similar to those found in the Danube Delta.

Marriage between the different nationalities and between immigrants and the original population led to a greater mix of population, but evidence of European roots is still strong in Uruguay. Many businesses are known by the name of the original founder and although Spanish is the official language, families still use their original language at home and make visits to their mother country when they can. But among young Uruguayans, there is a strong attachment and pride in their country. Some leave looking for better employment elsewhere, but many return, nostalgic for their country and their family.

THE GAUCHOS

When Charles Darwin, author of *The Origin of Species*, visited Uruguay in 1832, he met some gauchos and wrote of them:

Gauchos, the cowboys of the South American pampa, came into being in the seventeenth century and were essential in the fight for independence.

"With their brightly-colored garments, great spurs clanking about their heels, and knives stuck as daggers (and often so used) at their waists, they look a very different race of men from what might be expected from their name of gauchos, or simple countrymen. Their politeness is excessive; they never drink their spirits without expecting you to taste it; but whilst making their exceedingly graceful bow, they seem quite as ready, if occasion offered, to cut your throat."

Gauchos came into being some two hundred years before Darwin visited Uruguay. They were men, perhaps outlaws or refugees, who ventured into the interior away from the safety of the coast. There they bred with the local Indians and developed a free and independent life-style working with the cattle herds. Cattle provided them with everything: food, transportation, and leather for saddles, clothing, sacks, and wineskins. Gauchos were tough, resilient, and brilliant horsemen, and in the wars of

Most gauchos use sheepskin fleece covers on their saddles for extra comfort.

independence they were at the heart of the fighting armies led by Artigas.

The traditional gaucho attire has not changed much over the years. The gaucho wears a broad-brimmed black hat, long-sleeved cotton shirt, baggy trousers called *bombachas*, and black leather boots. He carries a poncho for use in cold weather and almost always has a mustache. He is never without his knife or *facón*, his most prized possession, which he tucks into his leather belt ready for use. Instead of the leathery bolas originally used for catching animals, the gaucho now prefers a lasso, which he can throw with great accuracy. Horses still have finely worked leather saddles, which the gaucho covers with sheepskin fleece for extra comfort.

There are signs of change, however, both in the gaucho dress, as bombachas give way to jeans, and in the life-style. Estancias, divided up over the generations and fenced in, are not as large and open as they were, and with good roads crossing the

A gaucho's life today is essentially the same as it was in the seventeenth century.

grasslands these great horsemen can no longer ride as freely as they used to. The work is still hard with long, lonely days in the grasslands mending fences, branding cattle, rounding up the herds, and tending the sheep before sundown, then returning to the estancia for a communal meal and dormitory-style living with the other gauchos. Many younger men now head for town life, encouraged by their families to look for easier ways to make a living.

But the gaucho will always be part of the folklore of both Uruguay and Argentina, and was immortalized as a romantic hero in the epic poem, *The Gaucho Martín Fierro*, written by José Hernández in 1872.

> A son am I of the rolling plain
> A gaucho born and bred
> And this is my pride; to live as free
> As the bird that cleaves the sky.

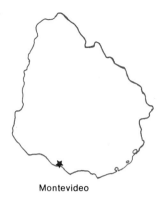

Montevideo

Chapter 6

EVERYDAY LIFE IN

URUGUAY

MONTEVIDEO

Montevideo, founded by Bruno Mauricio de Zabala in 1726, is the heart of Uruguay. It is the political, cultural, economic, commercial, and social hub of the republic. It is the country's only large port, handling 90 percent of all imports and exports, and the terminus for all transport from the interior. Just under half the population live in greater Montevideo, which covers an area of about 200 square miles (518 square kilometers).

Behind the city stands a hill, no more than 500 feet (152 meters) high, from which, it is claimed, the city takes its name. In the days of the early mariners, when there was no city, the hill became a welcome landmark on the otherwise flat coastline. The story goes that one member of the crew, sailing with Magellan in the sixteenth century, on sighting the hill shouted, *"Monte vide eu!"* ("I see a hill!"). On the top of the hill, or the *cerro*, as it is known, is an old fort, now a military museum, and the oldest lighthouse in the country, dating from 1804.

The colonial part of the city — including the cathedral, built in 1790; the *Cabildo*, or town hall, built in 1804; and the oldest

Opposite page: Montevideo is the capital and most important city in Uruguay. El Cerro Fortress (top) overlooks the harbor.

The Plaza Independencia with the Palacio Salvo in the center of the picture

square, Plaza Constitución—lies close to the docks. Nearby, the old port market building, losing none of its charm, has been converted into restaurants and outdoor cafés, which at lunchtime are filled with office workers. This is still the financial and business center of Montevideo where old balconied buildings house the well-established shipping firms, banks, and import and export companies. Also in this zone is the magnificent building of the Bank of the Republic that would do justice to any world financial center.

French, Italian, and other European styles influenced the city builders in the late 1800s and early 1900s around what is now the main square, the Plaza Independencia, and the principal shopping street, the Avenida 18 de Julio. In Plaza Independencia there is a life-size statue of General Artigas above the underground mausoleum in which he is buried. On one side of the square stands the extraordinary Palacio Salvo, Montevideo's first high

Shops along Avenida 18 de Julio (left)
and a woman feeding pigeons in a public park

building that is constructed in a highly ornate style. Another remarkable landmark not far from the plaza is the Legislative Palace, built entirely in native marble and one of the most lavish public buildings anywhere in South America.

East of the central city and extending along the coast and fine beaches are the modern residential suburbs with formal gardens and tree-lined roads. Indeed trees and parks are a special feature in Montevideo because space has never been a problem. Many of the parks, also influenced by European landscape gardeners, are a pleasure to visit with their rolling lawns, trees, and lakes and also provide leisure facilities for the families of Montevideo. In one, the Prado, there is a rose garden planted with 850 varieties of roses and the Municipal Museum of Fine Arts and History, while the largest park, the Rodó, has a boating lake, a children's playground, and the National Museum of Fine Arts with works by living artists. Nearby are the Zoological Gardens, and within

Scenes of Montevideo, from top:
A side street near the port, an aerial view
of the docks on the Río de la Plata, a fruit market,
and a view down Avenida Libertad
to the Legislative Palace

Montevideo, clockwise from left: A hardware store in a residential area, Solís Theater, Pocitos Beach, and a downtown plaza

A new shopping center under construction in Pocitos (left), a suburb of Montevideo, and slums on the outskirts of the city (right)

the grounds is a planetarium that is one of the best in South America. But perhaps the most impressive feature of the parks is the number of fine bronze statues by some of Uruguay's leading sculptors.

Montevideo now possesses its first large, modern shopping center in the suburb of Pocitos, but the downtown shopping streets are still popular and crowded, especially during the long, warm summer evenings when it is difficult to find an empty table in the outdoor cafés. Montevideans also enjoy regular Sunday markets where stalls are piled high with fresh fruit, flowers, clothing, old books, antiques, and countless bric-à-brac.

Despite the easygoing nature of the city, there are problems. Resources have been lacking in recent years to maintain buildings and property in good order, and parts of the city appear very run down. There is not enough money to repair the roads and pavements and at times the authorities have been unable to provide basic urban services like refuse collection, leaving rubbish to rot in the streets.

Women selling hand-crafted jewelry (left) and patrons at an outdoor restaurant

URUGUAYANS AT WORK

With such a high percentage of the people living in Montevideo, it is not surprising that over 87 percent of the population is urban. People are leaving the countryside because the medical and educational facilities they need for their families are not available. The majority head for the capital, but others have settled in Salto and Paysandú on the Uruguay River, as well as in the smaller towns closer to the coast such as Minas and Canelones.

There is a limit to the number of jobs available in the cities, and many people are unemployed. New arrivals turn their hands to whatever they can, doing odd jobs, sweeping streets, cleaning shoes, or setting up stalls in the main streets to sell trinkets or confections. Employed people often are engaged in service industries such as garages and restaurants. Eating out is a favorite pastime, and there are a great many bars, cafés, and restaurants, but never a shortage of waiters. Nor is there a shortage of taxis, as driving a taxi is a job that many can do provided they have a car.

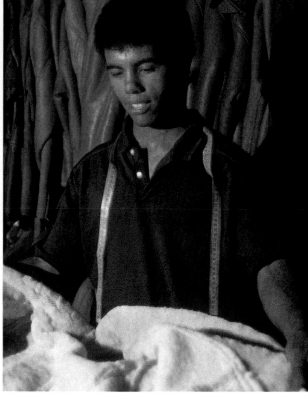

*Construction workers (above) and
an employee in a leather factory (right)*

Frequently two or more drivers will share a taxi so that it can be
kept in use twenty-four hours a day. In Montevideo skilled and
semiskilled workers are employed in construction and in
manufacturing industries that produce textiles, processed foods,
cement, and other goods.

A number of people work in the leather trade, many in small
factories making items of clothing, bags, and shoes for both the
domestic and the tourist market.

Cruise liners dock in Montevideo several times each year
bringing people of all nationalities in search of a bargain.

As in any country in the world, Uruguay's city dwellers include
shopkeepers, office workers, and people involved in commerce,
but the single biggest employer is the government, at great cost to
the economy. There are also lawyers, teachers, and doctors, but

In the south many people are employed in sheep farming and in the vineyards.

entry to these professions depends on a university-level education.

In the rural community, relatively few people work on the large estancias in the north and central part of the country. Often estancia owners are absent and leave the running of the farm to a manager who lives there with his family and the gauchos. The majority of people in agricultural work live in the south where they are employed on sheep farms or in vineyards, or they run their own family concern. A typical family may have about seven acres (three hectares), in which they produce grapes for sale to the vineyards or a selection of fruit and vegetables for the markets. Every member of the family helps to work on the land, including children and grandparents, as there is little modern machinery and often only a horse to pull a plow.

High school students in Montevideo entering their school

EDUCATION

The education reforms introduced by José Pedro Varela in 1877 and President Batlle y Ordóñez meant that early in the twentieth century the educational system in Uruguay was far in advance of most other South American nations. As a result the literacy rate is higher than in most countries in the Americas, with over 97 percent of the population able to read and write.

Today schooling is free and compulsory for children between the ages of six and fourteen. It is a considerable achievement that over 90 percent of pupils reach the sixth grade. Some schools are private and charge tuition, but most are run by the state, which also pays for the 5 percent of students who progress to the university level. The University of the Republic in Montevideo has schools of humanities, sciences, and engineering, as well as a distinguished school of medicine.

Although Uruguay can be proud of its educational record,

On a street in Montevideo (above) the homes and apartments appear to be quite similar, while in other areas the homes show more individuality (left).

teaching standards suffered under the military regime that took control in 1973. Suspecting that the universities were engaged in subversive activities, the military dismissed over half of the university staff. Teachers who had been active in political parties before 1973 were barred from holding teaching posts and were replaced by supporters of the military.

HOUSING

Most homes in Uruguay are built of brick or concrete blocks, as these materials are readily available. But the styles of houses range from the very simple to the luxurious. A typical family home in the country or small town is one story and has several rooms furnished plainly but adequately. Some open onto a small courtyard or patio, shaded by vines and adorned with flowers, where families take a siesta or just relax. Cooking is done on an open wood fire or cast-iron range or, where supplies of bottled gas

Contrasting architecture in a wealthy residential section of Montevideo

can be obtained, on a stove. Most homes in the towns have running water, but in the rural areas many families must rely on wells and windmill pumps.

An estancia house on the other hand, although also a one-story building, is usually large and rambling, with white stucco walls and a tiled or corrugated metal roof. The roof projects out beyond the walls to form a veranda all the way round, which is often covered by a profusion of flowers. Near the house there usually is a vegetable garden and small orchard. Isolated in open grasslands, the estancia house is surrounded by high trees—maybe a grove of eucalyptus, jacaranda, or palms. Other small houses for the farm workers, barns for shearing and storing wool, stables for horses, and sheds for cattle are nearby.

In Montevideo and Punta del Este high-rise apartment blocks now break into the skyline. They are modern, functional, and, in Punta del Este, very up-to-date. The housing needs of Punta del

Este are different from those of the rest of Uruguay, as everything is geared toward the tourist or vacationer. Some of the houses are better described as luxury mansions; other houses, smaller but individually styled and many with thatch roofs reminiscent of Europe, are attractively located in secluded pinewoods on the outskirts of the city.

In total contrast to the affluence of the Punta del Este developments, makeshift shacks have begun to appear on the outskirts of Montevideo. Constructed of wood or flattened oilcans and with no modern amenities, they are home for new arrivals with nowhere to go.

HEALTH AND THE WELFARE STATE

Based on the progressive ideas of Batlle y Ordóñez early in the twentieth century, Uruguay has been renowned for the development of its welfare state. Social security legislation provides for unemployment, injury sustained by workers, sickness, maternity and child allowances, and help for the old and needy. The welfare system is financed by contributions from workers, employers, and the government, but owing to economic decline these commitments have been difficult to maintain. Although there is estimated to be one doctor per 341 inhabitants, keeping the hospitals and medical services well equipped is also a financial problem, and people living in the countryside may have to wait many hours for assistance in an emergency.

Fortunately Uruguay has healthy citizens. Diseases such as smallpox, yellow fever, and malaria have either been eliminated or are under control. The annual increase in population is small and infant mortality is low. The life expectancy of seventy-two

Above: Milk and other dairy products are delivered in a horse-drawn wagon. Left: A butcher at work in a meat processing plant.

years is exceptional among South American countries. But this gives rise to another problem for the government—how to find more money to help the elderly and retired.

Uruguayans also enjoy good health because there is plenty of food produced locally, and most people can enjoy a nutritious and balanced diet. The consumption of meat is one of the highest in the world, and although beef is still most popular, in the rural areas mutton is now the staple diet—cooked in a variety of original ways. Meat is so much a part of the way of life that the government is under pressure to keep the price down and, for those who cannot afford meat, local authorities run food kitchens at subsidized prices. An early morning visit to the market in Montevideo reveals not only the abundance of meat but also a wonderful display of cheese and other dairy products. Crates of

Uruguayans carry hot water for their yerba maté in vacuum flasks.

fresh fruit and vegetables are brought in daily from the surrounding farms. In some parts of Montevideo and in most of the smaller towns, milk is delivered regularly in an old-fashioned horse and cart.

FOOD

An unusual custom that Uruguayans share with their neighbors in Paraguay and Argentina is the drinking of *yerba maté*. Yerba maté is a tea brewed from leaves of a tree related to the holly. The leaves, which are first dried and then finely powdered, are mixed in a *maté*, or gourd, with hot or cold water, and sipped through a *bombilla*, a metal (often silver) straw. The custom originated with

A tempting variety of sausages for sale

the native Indians who believed the bitter tea had magical and religious properties. It was taken up by the gauchos and, because of its vitamin content, has been described as one reason why the Uruguayans remained comparatively healthy throughout the wars for independence. Limited initially to the rural population, the custom is now widespread and people sip their yerba maté at all times of the day, whether working or relaxing. It is not uncommon to see a person walking in the street, a cup of maté in one hand and a vacuum flask under the arm filled with hot water to make more whenever necessary.

One of the greatest experiences Montevideo has to offer is a visit to the port market at lunchtime. Housed in one converted market building are a number of *parrilladas*, or grills, which make the most typical form of restaurant food in Uruguay. A parrillada is similar to a barbecue, but on a much grander scale. Metal grills propped at an angle over beds of glowing charcoal embers can easily be 30 square feet (2.8 square meters) and are covered with a huge variety of meats. Among the most popular cuts are *asado de*

Mercado de la Abundancia, *"Market of Abundance," in Montevideo*

tira, ribs; *pulpa*, beef without bones; and *lomo*, or fillet steak. If something other than beef is desired, there is a choice of pork, mutton, veal, and sometimes, chicken—all in large portions. Fitted in alongside the ribs are great spirals of spicy sausages known as *chorizos, morcillas, salchichas*, and *morcilla dulce*, which is a black sausage that includes orange peel and walnuts in the ingredients. Sausages cooked on small grills also are sold in the streets and plazas from modern, shiny aluminum-sided kiosks. Other snacks include hot dogs, *chivitos* or steakburgers, and sandwiches or croissants filled with ham and cheese. Fish, while not so popular as meat, is eaten in stews known as *cazuelas*.

The ready supply of good, fresh food means there is little demand for prepacked or fast food, although pizzas are popular. Montevideo has a number of cosmopolitan restaurants—in part a result of early immigrant influence—serving Italian, Chinese, Armenian, Arabic, and other dishes, and *confiterias* or tea shops with a mouth-watering supply of sugary pastries. One of the best known is outside Montevideo, in Minas. Two brothers, grandsons of a Basque immigrant who bought the firm in 1898, run the confiteria and have a reputation for making the best sweets in Uruguay. Their specialties include *yema*, an egg candy; *damasquito*, apricot sweets; and *cerranitos*, chocolate mounds.

RELIGION

In common with all the republics of South America, Uruguay became a Catholic country as a result of the work of Spanish missionaries and priests. But in Uruguay the missionaries stayed for a relatively short time and there are no buildings to compare with the beautiful churches and golden altars built by the Spaniards in the Andean countries and Argentina. Catholicism already was less strong in Uruguay than elsewhere on the continent when the British and other nationalities introduced alternative religions early in the nineteenth century. For most of that century the church was allied to the Blanco party who were not politically successful, and when Batlle y Ordóñez proposed the separation of church and state, there was little opposition.

Today in Uruguay there is complete freedom to practice any religion, and Evangelical, Baptist, Methodist, and other Protestant congregations are represented. The Catholic church does run some schools, has encouraged the formation of social and youth clubs, and several missions continue to do good works. But religion is not an important aspect of daily life and it is not taught in state schools. Marriage can take place outside the church, divorce is relatively easy and fairly common, and in some remote parts of the country there are no churches. Even major religious holidays are now known by other names. Christmas is "Family Day" and Easter is an official seven-day holiday called "Criollo Week."

Chapter 7

ARTS AND LEISURE

Unlike many countries in South America, Uruguay does not have a rich colonial heritage. It produced no great works of literature or art, and there are few examples of colonial churches or other buildings remaining today. The gauchos had their music—romantic songs and verse accompanied by guitars—which they played for their own pleasure, but these were never written down. During the wars for independence, support for the opposing factions also was expressed in song and verse, raising the spirits of the fighters with themes of revolution and liberty. Some of the best known of these verses, known as *gauchesque* poetry, were written not by gauchos but by rural and city dwellers in their admiration for the men on horseback. The most famous Uruguayan poet of this period was Bartolomé Hidalgo, a Montevideo bartender.

Independence in Uruguay was followed by an exchange of ideas with European countries that had not been possible under Spanish rule. When the immigrants arrived they brought with them traditions of their own culture, and in 1856 the grand Solís Theater was built in Montevideo. It is still the country's main theater, with regular performances by national and international companies.

In the last half of the nineteenth century, cultural expression in Uruguay developed in two forms. Some writers and artists were influenced by the literary and artistic ideas of Europe, while others looked to their own land for inspiration.

LITERATURE

The founder of modern literature in Uruguay, sometimes known as "the poet of the fatherland," was Juan Zorrilla de San Martín. He was born in 1855 and died in 1931. A flamboyant character in dress and appearance, he gained a reputation for reciting one of his own compositions, a patriotic poem called "La Leyenda Patria," whenever he attended important ceremonies. He wrote poetry and prose, and his works contain nationalistic ideas and, at the same time, express the European ideals of freedom and individuality. This combination of thought is perhaps best expressed in his masterpiece of verse, "Tabaré," written in 1879; this is a long romantic poem about the native Indians. His best-known prose work was written in praise of the independence hero, General Artigas.

The turn of the century was the golden age of Uruguayan literature. The progressive economic and political situation caused many writers to adopt new ideas. A literary movement developed in Latin America, called *Modernismo*, which corresponded broadly

Juan Carlos Onetti has received international acclaim for his writing. In 1980 Spain awarded him the Miguel de Cervantes literary prize.

with the integration of Spanish America into the world economy. These years were marked by an increase in international trade, a greater desire for consumer goods, and the emergence of a middle class searching for its own identity. The greatest exponent of Modernismo in Uruguay was Julio Herrera y Reissig who, with a group of Bohemian poets, had considerable influence in literary circles elsewhere in South America. Another group known as the Realists produced works that were regional and naturalistic, and generally concerned with the relationship between man and the earth. One of Uruguay's best-known dramatists, Florencio Sánchez, was a Realist. So too was Horacio Quiroga, who wrote short stories dealing with local rural life.

Early in the twentieth century, at the time the United States became commercially active in the region, some writers, like José Enrique Rodó, became conscious of the gap that existed between South America and its prosperous northern neighbor. In his work,

Ariel, he questioned the pursuit of technical progress and the material vlaues of North American democracy, while urging Latin Americans to create their own spirit. Although his approach to the subject was rather refined, tending to ignore the spirit of the gaucho or the Indian, it caused considerable debate at the time.

Literature has continued to play an important part in Uruguayan culture in recent years. There have been distinguished poets such as the popular Juana de Ibarbourou and Carlos Sabat Ercasty. Novelists who have received international acclaim include Juan Carlos Onetti, who wrote *No-Man's Land* and *The Shipyard,* and Mario Benedetti. Another writer who is widely read is Eduardo Galeano, who is compared by some to Onetti.

ART

The greatest artist of nineteenth-century Uruguay was Juan Manuel Blanes. Born in 1830 of a Spanish father and Argentine mother, he left school at the age of eleven and taught himself to draw. Later in life when his talents had been recognized, he received funds to study in Europe. He is best remembered for his meticulous paintings depicting the history of the Río de la Plata region, which include portraits of military heroes and paintings of gauchos, sometimes on very small canvases.

While the nineteenth century was dominated by the talent of Blanes, so the twentieth century belongs to two great, universally acclaimed artists, Pedro Figari and Joaquín Torres García. Both men were remarkable, not just as artists, but for their many, varied talents. Figari was born of Italian parents and in 1886 began a professional career as a lawyer, publisher, and journalist. He wrote on many subjects including law, education, and poetry and he founded the newspaper *El Diario.* In 1896 he entered

Above: El Palito, *"Gaucho Dance," by Pedro Figari*
Right: Joaquín Torres García's painting used
symbols (a fish, a clock, etc.) to make this composition.

politics and eight years later was appointed vice-president. In 1915 he became the director of the School of Fine Arts and Crafts in Montevideo. After two years he was forced to resign from this post due to opposition to some radical educational and artistic reforms he suggested. It was only then that he seriously took up painting. He studied in Europe with Postimpressionists and his work is easily recognizable for its soft colors and rural scenes depicted with much charm and character. He concentrated on landscapes of the Río de la Plata region, social gatherings, and scenes of everyday life. Today his work is in great demand.

Joaquín Torres García was born in Montevideo of a Spanish father and a Uruguayan mother. He spent forty years of his life outside Uruguay, but his influence on his native country has been enormous. From the age of seventeen Torres García studied in Spain and among his early works were stained-glass windows and frescoes for churches in Barcelona and a series of murals in the city's Provincial Government building. After a short stay in New York, he returned to Paris where, in 1928, he collaborated with other artists to organize the first international exhibition of

Carlos Páez Vilaró talks to his assistants (left) as they work on the mural in the Pan American Union tunnel. One of Vilaró's sculptures stands at the entrance to his house (right).

abstract art. Returning to Montevideo in 1933 he continued to work on the art form most associated with his name: Constructivism. Constructivism is a form of abstract art using signs and symbols and a variety of materials, including wire, glass, and metal. He established an art school and the Association of Constructivist Art, published many articles and books, and in 1944 he founded his studio, the Taller Torres-García. A lasting memorial to his work is the Cosmic Monument, a free-standing wall containing many of the symbols and signs used in his paintings, which he erected in Rodó Park in Montevideo.

Successful contemporary artists include José Gamarra and Carlos Páez Vilaró. Vilaró is particularly well known for the mural he completed in 1960 in the tunnel connecting the two buildings of the Pan American Union in Washington, D.C. Painted in oil and 525 feet (160 meters) long, it is said to be the longest mural in the world. In recent years he has concentrated

The life-size bronze, La Carreta, *by José Belloni*

mainly on ceramics and sculpture, and exhibits of his work can be
seen in Casapueblo, the extraordinary Spanish-Moroccan house
he has built on a cliff at Punta Ballena near Punta del Este.

SCULPTURE

Sculpture, like literature and painting, has been influenced by
foreign artists but many of the impressive statues and sculptures
in Uruguay portray figures of national importance or subjects
significant in the history of the republic. There are a number of
bronze sculptures in Montevideo's parks, including *The Last of the
Charrúas* by Prati. Two of the most remarkable are by Uruguay's
best-known sculptor, José Belloni. *La Carreta* in the Batlle y
Ordóñez Park is a life-size bronze of three yoke of oxen drawing a
wagon, guided by a man on a horse, while *La Diligence* depicts a
full-size stagecoach and horses.

La Diligence *by Belloni (above) and* El Gaucho
by José Louis Zorrilla de San Martín (right)

Most visitors to Montevideo are impressed by the figure of *El
Gaucho*, a gaucho on horseback with his lance and his poncho
fluttering in the wind, which stands at the end of the Avenida 18
de Julio. It is the work of José Luis Zorrilla de San Martín, son of
the writer, and was erected as a tribute to all gauchos who died in
the cause of freedom. At the base of the statue are four bas-reliefs
of typical rural scenes.

LEISURE

A popular form of relaxation, particularly during the winter
months, is the cinema. Uruguay has a small filmmaking industry,
but most movies are imported from the United States and Europe.
For those who prefer theater, there are productions of drama,
ballet, and opera presented at the Solís Theater and by a number
of smaller companies in the capital. Musical entertainment ranges

A movie theater in Montevideo

from classical, given by Montevideo's symphony and chamber orchestras, to occasional pop concerts staged in the Rodó park.

Carnivals just before the beginning of Lent and Easter week are two of the main holidays when most of the country comes to a standstill. At Carnival time, groups of up to fifty or more dancers and drummers parade in costume in the streets of Montevideo. Some of the dances and songs, known as *candombe*, have their roots in the African slaves of the Río de la Plata region. During Easter week there are rodeos, horse-breaking, stunts by cowboys, large festival *asados* or barbecues, and dances. Some folk songs and dances such as the *milonga* and *perícon* have survived, particularly in rural areas, since early colonial days.

In the summertime, Uruguayan families have a wonderful choice of beaches where they can relax. Montevideo alone has nine beaches extending along the coast, including Pocitos, the best known. During the holiday season the beaches around Punta del

Pocitos Beach

Este are always crowded, but there are other very attractive bays not far from the capital that are less developed and good for swimming.

Vacations near the beach, or even in the interior, allow Uruguayan families to indulge in two of their most popular pastimes: camping and fishing. When they go camping, Uruguayans make sure they are well equipped and comfortable, and the colorful tents of the campers are easy to spot among the well-laid-out campsites in the pine forests of the coast and in the hills. Large barbecues are an essential part of camping life, often with meat and fish on the menu. People love to fish, usually with a rod and line from the riverbank or from bridges, and will spend many hours sipping maté and chatting with friends while waiting for a catch.

SPORT

There are facilities and opportunities for many sports in Uruguay. In the river estuaries and off the coast there are water skiing, surfing, and diving. There are clubs for yachting, sailing, and rowing; an Olympic-size swimming pool in Montevideo; and golf courses of international standard. Horse riding and show jumping are popular and the race course of Maronas is very well attended. Other sports include tennis, basketball, hockey, and cycling, but the two most associated with Uruguay are soccer (called *futbol*) and polo. Polo matches take place regularly in Punta del Este, often against teams from Argentina with whom there is great competition, and occasionally against international teams from Europe.

As in every country in South America, soccer is easily the most popular sport, for everyone has the opportunity to play. The game was introduced to Uruguay by British residents and the crews of British warships at the end of the nineteenth century. Uruguayan teams were Olympic champions in 1924 and 1928.

All games attract large crowds, but particularly the World Cup games. This competition is very special to Uruguayans who were the first to host the Cup games, in 1930, when they won. They were world champions again in 1950, and whenever qualifying competitions take place now, people who cannot squeeze into the country's main stadium, the Centenario in Montevideo, stop work to watch television or listen to the radio.

Uruguay's main exports have traditionally
been based on the cattle and sheep industries.

Chapter 8

THE ECONOMY TODAY

Together with Argentina and Chile, Uruguay's economy in the late nineteenth and early twentieth centuries was well in advance of other countries in South America. There was considerable prosperity and both in Montevideo and the interior, people enjoyed a high standard of living. In recent years the economy has faced considerable difficulties. Traditionally the country's main exports have always been based on the cattle and sheep industries. At certain times, as during the two world wars, the demand for leather, meat, and wool has been high and export earnings good. But since World War II, with the exception of a short boom during the Korean War in the 1950s, demand and the world price for these items have declined. And Uruguay has few alternative industries that can help boost export earnings.

Other factors beyond the control of the government also have affected the economy. In 1988-89 large parts of the north and northeast of Uruguay suffered a drought that severely damaged crops and caused the deaths of thousands of cattle. Some 650,000 had to be killed during the first four months of 1989, which was 50 percent more than in the same period in the previous year. Hydroelectric output was reduced, and at Salto Grande only two of the fourteen turbines were working due to the low level of the Uruguay River. Food and other essential goods were in short supply, and television transmission was limited to four hours each night.

Conditions in neighboring Brazil and Argentina also have an influence on Uruguay's economy. In 1989, as a result of a currency crisis in Argentina, so many millions of dollars were transferred into Uruguay that it doubled the amount of money in circulation in the country. The effect of this, together with the drought, was to push the already high rate of inflation even higher–to around 80 percent by the end of the year. Matters were made worse for Uruguay's workers as the government determined to limit wage increases. The same year, however, there was a record drop in the unemployment figure, to 7.8 percent–the lowest in recent years. By 1992 inflation was 58 percent.

LIVESTOCK

Fertile soil, a mild climate, plenty of water, and extensive grasslands are the important factors behind Uruguay's livestock economy. Over 85 percent of the land is given over to pastures for cattle and sheep, with just 10 to 12 percent devoted to agriculture. According to official figures in 1991, there were over nine million cattle, and thirty million sheep. Beef cattle are mainly Herefords, and sheep include breeds such as Corriedale, valued for its meat, and crossbreeds for their wool. Uruguay used to be second only to Argentina as a meat and meat-product

Wool from sheep (and there are many sheep) is one of Uruguay's principal exports.

exporter. Unfortunately these exports were affected by a drop in demand, particularly when the European Community, once a major meat importer, began exporting its own meat. Also in the early 1980s, the beef-cattle sector suffered from low world prices. The number of sheep, however, rose in the 1980s reflecting higher prices paid for wool.

Wool is now the principal export, followed by meat and hides. Together they account for about 35 percent of export earnings.

Milk, butter, cheese, poultry, and pigs are produced largely for the domestic market but exports of some dairy products are increasing in importance.

AGRICULTURE

Agricultural farming began with the arrival of the European immigrants in the nineteenth century, but makes only a limited contribution to export revenue. Most of the small farms are

The windmill on this farm is used to pump water.

concentrated in the coastal region, but sugar is grown in the
north, and rice, the only cereal to be exported, is cultivated almost
entirely in the northeast. Other crops include wheat, maize,
barley, oats, sorghum, potatoes, oilseeds such as sunflower and
linseed, cotton, and tobacco. Some cereals and oilseeds are
cultivated in the departments of Río Negro and Paysandú along
the Uruguay River. There is a wide variety of vegetables and
grapes, oranges, lemons, apples, pears, quinces, melons, apricots,
figs, and chestnuts are among the many fruits grown. The grapes
are the basis of a small wine industry that has developed around
the frontier towns of Bella Unión, Rivera, and Artigas, and in the
southern part of the country.

Traditionally, agriculture has always taken second place to
cattle and sheep because the better land is put to grazing. There is
little investment in new machinery and now many people are
leaving rural areas because it is hard for the small farmer to make
a living.

A country lane lined with eucalyptus trees

FISHING AND FORESTRY

Despite its long coastline, Uruguay has only a small fishing industry. Efforts have been underway since early in the 1970s to develop the potential of the rich offshore fishing grounds, and in the first ten years there was a dramatic increase in exports. Prior to 1973 Uruguay had not exported fish, but in that year export sales reached about one million dollars. By 1980 export sales rose to about fifty million dollars with markets in twenty-three countries.

In recent years exports have fluctuated and there is still not much demand for fish in the local market. State-owned organizations continue to promote the industry, and there is a fish-meal plant in La Paloma. Industries have insufficient funds and equipment to exploit the potential of this rich resource.

There is very little natural forest in the country, and although some reforestation of eucalyptus and conifers has been carried out, Uruguay is dependent on wood imports from Brazil for industrial and consumer use.

101

GALLINAS SCHOOL LIBRARY
177 N. San Pedro Road
San Rafael CA 94903

The bottling plant in Minas (left); a shop selling clocks
set into rocks that are cut in the shape of Uruguay (right)

MANUFACTURING

About one-quarter of Uruguay's working people are employed
in construction and manufacturing industries, most of which are
based in Montevideo. The older industries are connected with
livestock and textiles. Refrigeration, when it was introduced early
in the twentieth century, added a new dimension to the meat-
packing and meat-exporting industries. Large refrigeration plants,
frigoríficos, were built to handle canned, frozen, and chilled meats,
and by-products. The principal manufacturing industries are still
the packing and processing of meat, fish, drinks, and sugar.

Connected to the cattle industry is the curing and tanning of
hides and the production of leather goods. The country's main
bottling plant in the small town of Minas was established in 1892
near the natural spring of Salus. The plant produces 23,000 bottles
an hour of mineral water and mineral water mixed with fruit
juices. There also are factories for textiles and cloth.

Medium-technology industries include oil refining; motor vehicle assembly; and manufacture of cement, chemicals, rubber and paper products, and electrical machinery. Recent governments have emphasized the development of export-oriented light industry and modernization of traditional industry. As the state, through organizations as ANCAP founded in 1931, has controlled much industry, the government is working on improved economy by measures such as tariff deregulation and privatization.

MINING AND ENERGY

Uruguay has no known mineral reserves, such as oil, coal, or uranium, of any significance. Exploration for oil has taken place but the results have been disappointing. There are known deposits of iron ore, gold, manganese, copper, zinc, and lead, which have either not been developed or development has been abandoned. Mineral activity is concentrated mainly in talc, which is exported to Argentina; quartz for the glass industry; marbles and granites, limestone and sandstone for the construction industry; and semiprecious stones such as agates, geodes, and amethysts. Several tourist shops in Montevideo have a fine display of these stones.

The republic's electricity comes from its four hydroelectric plants, which now produce sufficient electricity for local use with a small surplus for export. The first to be built, the station at Rincón del Bonete, was completed on the Río Negro in 1945. The dam at Salto on the Uruguay River was constructed jointly by Uruguay and Argentina and first generated electricity in 1979. The construction, which made the Uruguay River navigable for an extra 89 miles (143 kilometers), also is designed to assist in flood control, irrigation, and the provision of drinking water. A large lake was formed behind the dam, stretching over 93.2 miles (150 kilometers) upstream, in which there now is experimental fish farming.

TOURISM

The tourist trade is an important source of foreign exchange. Most of the tourists come from other South American countries— mainly Argentina. It is an easy journey to cross the Río de la Plata by ferry or hydrofoil, and from Colonia or Montevideo it is a short drive to Punta del Este, the center of tourism on the coast.

In Punta del Este the government has invested in modern hotels, apartments, and vacation homes. The beaches are excellent for swimming and facilities are available for all kinds of sport and entertainment. There are regular excursions to Lobos Island to see the seal colonies, and to Gorriti Island, which is densely wooded and has superb beaches and some remnants from colonial days. In the season from December to the end of February, it is virtually impossible to find an empty room—even in Maldonado, which is now a suburb of Punta del Este. But out of season, any tourists can have a resort almost to themselves.

Between Montevideo and Punta del Este there are other major resorts such as Atlántida, Piriápolis, and Portezuelo, with the nearby beautiful crescent-shaped beach of Punta Ballena. Other developments are under way all along the coast.

Although the coast is the main center of tourism, Argentines also take their vacations along the Uruguay River where there are small yachting harbors and excellent camping facilities.

Chapter 9

URUGUAY AND
THE WORLD

TRADING WITH THE WORLD

Since 1986, when there was an increased demand, exports have improved and in 1988 Uruguay recorded a good trade surplus on its balance of payments. The export of wool in 1988 increased by 36 percent over the previous year, with China the principal importer, followed by the Soviet Union. Total exports exceeded imports by almost three hundred million dollars. The republic's principal trading partners for exports and imports are Brazil, Argentina, the United States, and the European Union, in particular Germany.

The trade surplus partly reflects the country's efforts to reduce imports, especially oil, which has been subject to considerable price increases. Other imports include machinery, electrical and transport equipment, minerals, metals, and chemicals, as well as a small percentage of food, drink, and tobacco products.

A good trading surplus is essential to help Uruguay repay its foreign debt. It is a major problem the republic shares with many other developing countries. In 1973, the world price of oil soared. For some countries who produced oil this was good news, but it left countries like Uruguay with an increasingly large import bill. A secondary effect was that banks in the United States and Europe suddenly had a surplus of dollars that they needed to put to good use. Large loans were offered to many third-world countries, which were already in debt to the World Bank, the International Monetary Fund, and private banks. In time it became obvious that a number of these countries could not afford to repay either the loan or the interest payments that had accrued. Since the mid-1980s, serious international attempts have been made to resolve the situation, and it was one of the first problems addressed by President Lacalle when he was elected in 1989. By early 1991 he was able to announce that an agreement had been reached in which interest rates had been significantly decreased, and with easier, longer-term repayments, the strain on Uruguay's economy was eased.

TRANSPORTATION

Montevideo is the hub of the country's transportation network. Most roads are paved, or all-weather with hard dirt surfaces that are frequently graded, but in country areas many of the minor roads connecting villages and small towns are little more than tracks with many potholes. Considerable improvements in the network were made between 1985 and 1989, and loans were received from the World Bank and the Inter-American Development Bank, totaling 165 million dollars, toward the modernization of major international routes and the construction of the new Route 1, which links Montevideo and Buenos Aires by way of Colonia and a ferry. It is the most important road in the country and is well used by commercial and tourist traffic.

Other routes, fanning out like spokes from a wheel, connect Montevideo to the rest of the country, Argentina, and Brazil. A

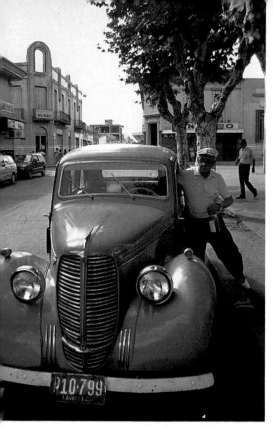

These vintage cars are a Hillman (far left), a Ford (top left), and a Chevrolet (bottom left).

good service of long-distance buses covers these routes comfortably and frequently, but it is possible and not at all unusual to drive along roads in the interior for many hours and not see another vehicle.

In Montevideo and other towns there are plenty of taxis, scooters, and bicycles, but other older forms of transportation still exist. Horses and carts are still widely used—less so in the capital, although garbage is sometimes collected in this way. In some areas horses and carts are used for delivering milk and other supplies or simply as a means of transportation. Electric trolley buses cover regular routes in Montevideo.

Most amazing, though, are the vintage cars (*cachilas*) that are commonplace in most towns in Uruguay. Many date back fifty years or more and include Fords, Chevrolets, Studebakers, and British cars of the 1950s. Economic necessity has forced the people of Uruguay to repair and maintain these old models, as imported new cars are too expensive. Younger people also prefer the older cars as they are cheaper to run, and the owners take pride in restoring the cars to their original condition. Sometimes parts from several vehicles create a curious hybrid model, often topped with a homemade wooden cabin. Another incentive in maintaining these old vehicles is that the cars are rapidly becoming collector's items, with an appreciating value. For the moment though, there are restrictions on the export of cachilas, and most will remain in Uruguay for the foreseeable future.

There are no passenger railways in Uruguay although trains still carry freight. In 1911, in proportion to the size of the republic, there were more miles of railway in Uruguay than in any other country in South America. The network was an essential part of opening up the country, which allowed for easy access between the interior and the coast and development of the economy. A British-owned company, the Central Uruguayan Railway, ran the network until after World War II when the railways were nationalized. The railway lines follow much the same routes as the roads, connecting Montevideo to interior and frontier towns.

Uruguay has a state airline, Pluna, which operates international and national flights, and Tamu, a branch of the Uruguayan air force that covers internal routes. Aero Uruguaya has cargo charter services to Europe, the United States, and destinations in South America. The main international airport of Carrasco is in Montevideo and is used by airlines of most other South American countries, and some European airlines such as Lufthansa and Air France.

Regular car ferries and passenger hydrofoil services run several times a day between Colonia and Buenos Aires, with the

Passengers boarding a Pluna Airlines Boeing 737

hydrofoils carrying one hundred passengers for the fifty-minute journey. Ferries also run the longer journey between Montevideo and Buenos Aires. Uruguay has a small merchant fleet, although it is presently not large enough to cope with the volume of freight transported in and out of the country. Instead the republic has to rely on international shipping, and the port of Montevideo which began efficiency reforms in 1992, is open to vessels from all over the world. The Río de la Plata estuary is considered by many nations to be an international waterway. Within the republic there are about 771 miles (1,240 kilometers) of navigable waters that provide an important means of transportation.

COMMUNICATION

Most newspapers in Uruguay are published in Montevideo and can be distributed easily and quickly across the country. Some towns in the interior, such as Florida, Minas, Paysandú, and Salto, have local publications, but their circulation is very limited. This

Secondhand book market in Montevideo

is another indication of the position and influence that the capital city has over the rest of the country. Many of the newspapers have a political background, such as *El Día*, founded by the Colorado president Batlle y Ordóñez. Pedro Figari, the artist and one-time vice-president, founded *El Diario*, now an evening paper, which reflects the more conservative, independent branch of the Colorado party. *La Mañana* is another newspaper with Colorado leanings, while *El País* supports the Partido Nacional and *La Hora Popular* is left wing. Major international news agencies, including Reuters and United Press International, are represented in Montevideo.

Due to the high literacy rate, Uruguay has a large reading public, and newspaper stands carry a wide range of national and international magazines specializing in hobbies, topics for women and children, political and social matters, agriculture, industry, and many other subjects. In markets and on street corners, there also is a lively trade in old and secondhand books. For most of its history Uruguay has enjoyed freedom of the press, although there was censorship during the period of military rule between 1973 and 1985.

Television and radio can be received in most parts of the country. There are four television stations in Montevideo and sixteen serving towns outside the capital, with forty radio stations in the capital and sixty in the rest of the country. Quite a high percentage of television programs are films brought in from the United States and Europe. For important world affairs, international news footage is relayed. Sports viewing is very popular, but family viewing is mostly taken up with *novelas*, or soap operas, which are shown nightly.

All forms of modern communication are available in Uruguay, although telex and facsimile machines are not easily found outside the towns. Uruguay can be dialed directly from outside the continent, and the international line is often better than a local call made from Montevideo to the interior. The telegraph service is widespread throughout the country.

ROLE IN THE WORLD

Uruguay has good relations with the rest of the world, and many nations have diplomatic representation in Montevideo. Also Uruguay has embassies in over fifty countries, including the Americas, Europe, the Middle and Far East, and Africa.

The republic's membership in organizations such as the World Bank, the Inter-American Development Bank, and the Organization of American States, among others, is related to financial and development considerations and Uruguay is often the location of international conferences. In 1980 the Treaty of Montevideo established the Latin American Integration

Association whose aim was to protect Latin-American trade in the face of world economic recession. More recently Uruguay was a meeting place for a round of talks of the General Agreement on Tariffs and Trade (GATT), which aimed to reach a compromise with the developed nations of the world and allow the developing countries better terms for trade.

An important recent development was the creation early in 1991 of a common market organization, called Mercosur, with Brazil, Argentina, Paraguay, and Uruguay. It will be operating gradually by 1995 and allow free trade between the four countries and set common tax duties for imports from outside regions. The Mercosur eventually will converge with the North American Free Trade Agreement (NAFTA). A further aim is to increase production and foreign investment. Uruguay will probably be chosen as the financial center of Mercosur.

THE FUTURE

Following the prosperity achieved in Uruguay in the early part of the twentieth century, recent years have not been happy ones for the tiny republic. The people, though still retaining their reputation as one of the friendliest nations in the hemisphere, are disillusioned with the failure of succeeding governments to improve the economic situation. Nonetheless there is cause for optimism.

The guerrilla movements of the 1960s and 1970s have been crushed, the military rule of 1973 to 1985 is a bad memory, but with President Sanguinetti's amnesty, the matter of reprisals is closed, and recent elections have confirmed the country's desire and ability to return to democratic rule.

Faces of Uruguay

Steps are being taken to diversify the country's economy, President Lacalle has addressed the foreign debt problem, and the new common market arrangements with South American neighbors give hope that the economic situation will improve.

Difficult years may still lie ahead, but as Uruguay approaches the twenty-first century, there is reason to believe that this gentle, pastoral land can and will enjoy peace and prosperity.

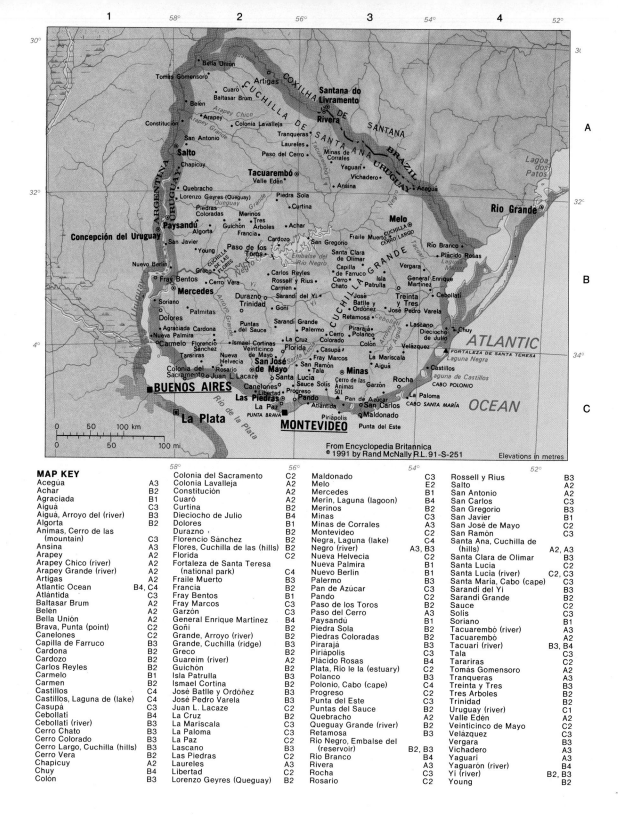

From Encyclopedia Britannica
© 1991 by Rand McNally R.L. 91-S-251

Elevations in metres

MAP KEY

Acegúa	A3
Achar	B2
Agraciada	B1
Aiguá	C3
Aiguá, Arroyo del (river)	B3
Algorta	B2
Animas, Cerro de las (mountain)	C3
Ansina	A3
Arapey	A2
Arapey Chico (river)	A2
Arapey Grande (river)	A2
Artigas	A2
Atlantic Ocean	B4, C4
Atlántida	C3
Baltasar Brum	A2
Belén	A2
Bella Unión	A2
Brava, Punta (point)	C2
Canelones	C2
Capilla de Farruco	B3
Cardona	B2
Cardozo	B2
Carlos Reyles	B2
Carmelo	B1
Carmen	B2
Castillos	C4
Castillos, Laguna de (lake)	C4
Casupá	C3
Cebollatí	B4
Cebollatí (river)	B3
Cerro Chato	B3
Cerro Colorado	B3
Cerro Largo, Cuchilla (hills)	B3
Cerro Vera	B2
Chapicuy	A2
Chuy	B4
Colón	B3
Colonia del Sacramento	C2
Colonia Lavalleja	A2
Constitución	A2
Cuaró	A2
Curtina	B2
Dieciocho de Julio	B4
Dolores	B1
Durazno	B2
Florencio Sánchez	B2
Flores, Cuchilla de las (hills)	B2
Florida	C2
Fortaleza de Santa Teresa (national park)	C4
Fraile Muerto	B3
Francia	B2
Fray Bentos	B1
Fray Marcos	B2
Garzón	C3
General Enrique Martínez	B4
Goñi	B2
Grande, Arroyo (river)	B2
Grande, Cuchilla (ridge)	B3
Greco	B2
Guareim (river)	A2
Guichón	B2
Isla Patrulla	B3
Ismael Cortina	B2
José Batlle y Ordóñez	B3
José Pedro Varela	B3
Juan L. Lacaze	C2
La Cruz	B2
La Mariscala	C3
La Paloma	C3
La Paz	C2
Lascano	B3
Las Piedras	C2
Laureles	A3
Libertad	C2
Lorenzo Geyres (Queguay)	B2
Maldonado	C3
Melo	E2
Mercedes	B1
Merín, Laguna (lagoon)	B4
Merinos	B2
Minas	C3
Minas de Corrales	A3
Montevideo	C2
Negra, Laguna (lake)	C4
Negro (river)	A3, B3
Nueva Helvecia	C2
Nueva Palmira	B1
Nuevo Berlín	B1
Palermo	B3
Pan de Azúcar	C3
Pando	C2
Paso de los Toros	B2
Paso del Cerro	A3
Paysandú	B1
Piedra Sola	B2
Piedras Coloradas	B2
Pirarajá	B3
Piriápolis	C3
Plácido Rosas	B4
Plata, Río de la (estuary)	C2
Polanco	B3
Polonio, Cabo (cape)	C4
Progreso	C2
Punta del Este	C3
Puntas del Sauce	B2
Quebracho	B2
Queguay Grande (river)	B2
Retamosa	B3
Río Branco	B4
Río Negro, Embalse del (reservoir)	B2, B3
Rivera	A3
Rocha	C3
Rosario	C2
Rossell y Rius	B3
Salto	A2
San Antonio	A2
San Carlos	C3
San Gregorio	B3
San Javier	B1
San José de Mayo	C2
San Ramón	C3
Santa Ana, Cuchilla de (hills)	A2, A3
Santa Clara de Olimar	B3
Santa Lucia	C2
Santa Lucia (river)	C2, C3
Santa María, Cabo (cape)	C3
Sarandí del Yi	B3
Sarandí Grande	B2
Sauce	C2
Solís	C3
Soriano	B1
Tacuarembó (river)	A3
Tacuarembó	A2
Tacuari (river)	B3, B4
Tala	C3
Tarariras	C2
Tomás Gomensoro	A2
Tranqueras	A3
Treinta y Tres	B3
Tres Arboles	B2
Trinidad	B2
Uruguay (river)	C1
Valle Edén	A2
Veinticinco de Mayo	C2
Velázquez	C3
Vergara	B3
Vichadero	A3
Yaguarí	A3
Yaguarón (river)	B4
Yi (river)	B2, B3
Young	B2

Gauchos are, as Charles Darwin wrote, "simple countrymen" and an integral part of Uruguay's folklore.

MINI-FACTS AT A GLANCE

GENERAL INFORMATION

Official Name: Republica Oriental del Uruguay (Eastern Republic of Uruguay).

Government: Uruguay's constitution, adopted in 1966 and restored in 1985, provides for a republican government. Executive power is held by the president, who is directly elected for a period of five years. The president is assisted by a vice-president and a Council of Ministers. Legislative power rests with the Congress, which is composed of a 30-member Senate and a 99-member Chamber of Deputies. The highest court is the five-member Supreme Court.

Language: Spanish is the official language, and nearly all Uruguayans speak Spanish. Portuguese is popular along the Brazil-Uruguay border.

National Flag: Approved in 1830, the flag has four azure blue horizontal stripes on a white background. These nine stripes represent the nine departments into which the country was originally divided after gaining independence. On a square white section on the hoist side is a golden sun with 16 rays (sometimes 20 rays are shown) alternately straight and wavy. The "Sun of May" symbolizes Uruguay's independence.

National Emblem: A quartered blue and white elliptical badge on which are displayed gold scales of justice and equality, the green cerro or mountain island of Montevideo, a dark brown stallion, and a gold longhorn bull. The badge is enclosed within olive and laurel branches tied at the base with a silver ribbon. The golden "Sun of May" rises over the top.

National Anthem: *Himno Nacional del Uruguay* ("National Hymn of Uruguay") begins "Orientales, la patria o la tumba" ("Easterners [Uruguayans] our country or death")

Money: One Uruguayan new peso is equal to 100 centesimos. In July 1994, one U.S. dollar was equal to 4.94 Uruguayan new pesos.

Weights and Measures: The metric system is the official standard, but some Spanish units also are used.

Population: 3,166,000 (1994 estimate); 86% urban, 14% rural. Density is 46 persons per sq. mi. (18 persons per sq km). Almost half of the population lives in the capital city of Montevideo.

Religion: Under the constitution church and state are separate and there is complete religious liberty. Uruguay has no official state religion. Some 60% of the population follows Roman Catholicism, but less than half of the adults attend church regularly.

Administrative Divisions: Uruguay is divided into 19 administrative departments for local government. Each department has an elected governor and legislature.

Area: 68,037 sq. mi. (176,215 sq km)

Cities:

Montevideo	1,500,000 *
Salto	77,400
Paysandú	75,200
Las Piedras	61,300
Rivera	55,400
Melo	39,600
Tacuarembó	38,600
Minas	33,700
Mercedes	33,300

(Population based on 1985 estimates)
* 1992 estimate

GEOGRAPHY

Highest Point: Mirador Nacional at 1,644 ft. (501 m)

Lowest point: Sea level

Rivers and Lakes: The Río de la Plata and the Uruguay River are the major rivers. The Río Negro flows through the heart of the lowlands, and along with its tributaries, its drainage area covers about 40% of the country. A dam on the Río Negro has resulted in the country's largest lake, *Lake Rincon del Bonete* behind the Dr. Gabriel Terra Dam. Laguna Merín in the northeast is the principal lagoon. An international bridge on the Uruguay River connects Paysandú with Colón in Argentina.

Forests: Some 4 percent of the land is forested. *Ombú*, resembling a small oak, is the best-known tree. Small woods of eucalyptus and pines can be found scattered across the grasslands. Acacias, yatay palms, *algarrobos*, "carob trees," and willows also are found along the rivers. The wood and bark from the *quebracho* tree is used in tanning and dyeing. There has been reforestation of conifers and eucalyptus.

Wildlife: Centuries of intensive cattle raising have resulted in the disappearance of certain wildlife species. Skunks, small wildcats, foxes, armadillos, pampas deer, hares, and opossums are some of the surviving mammals. Otters, capybaras, and sea lions are found in the coastal region and on nearby islands.

Birds: Bird life on the grasslands, swamps, and along the riverbanks is rich and varied. Swallows, parrots, cowbirds, wrens, *horneos* or "oven birds," rheas, owls, herons, *jacanas* or "lily trotters," red-legged seriemas, the tinamous, and the *teros* or southern lapwings are the most common birds.

Climate: Uruguay has a temperate, mild, and humid climate with an average winter temperature of 57° F. to 61° F. (14° C to 16° C) in July, and an average summer temperature of 70° F. to 82° F. (21° C to 28° C) in January. Freezing temperatures are almost unknown. Uruguay receives some 40 in. (102 cm) of rain annually. The wettest months are April and May. As the country lies south of the equator, its seasons are opposite those in the Northern Hemisphere.

Greatest Distance: North to south—330 mi. (530 km)
East to west—280 mi. (450 km)

ECONOMY AND INDUSTRY

Agriculture: Less than 10% of the area is under cultivation. Some of the large *estancias* "estates" have been divided up into family farms. The average farm is about 250 acres (101 hectares), but some large ranches cover more than 5,000 acres (2,024 hectares). Chief crops are wheat, rice, sugarcane, sugar beets, oats, oilseeds, cotton, tobacco, potatoes, sorghum, sunflowers, maize, and barley. Principal fruits are grapes, peaches, oranges, lemons, apples, melons, apricots, figs, tangerines, chestnuts, and pears. The fish catch includes hake, weakfish, croaker, and anchovy, but there is very little local demand for fish.

Livestock: Uruguay is primarily a pastoral country where large areas are devoted to extensive livestock grazing. Almost 90% of the farm area is used for cattle raising and traditionally is Uruguay's major economic activity. Livestock provides almost one-half of the total export earnings. Wool is the principal export, followed by meat and hides. There are about 39 million beef cattle and sheep. Chief livestock products are milk, butter, beef and veal, wood, mutton and lamb, cattle hides, poultry, sheepskins, and eggs.

Mining: Uruguay does not have mineral reserves of any economic significance. Small quantities of building materials such as gravel, sand, marble, granite, and limestone are extracted. There are small deposits of gold, copper, manganese, zinc, lead, talc, iron ore, and semiprecious stones such as agate and amethyst. There are no known natural gas reserves, and oil and coal reserves are very small.

Manufacturing: Most of the manufacturing industries are based in Montevideo. The older industries are connected with livestock products. Large refrigeration plants handle canned, frozen, and chilled meats and by-products. Major manufacturing products are wine, sugar, cigarettes, foodstuffs, chemicals, footwear, leather apparel, tires, cement, textiles, clothes, fuel oils, and kerosene.

Transportation: Uruguay is well connected by roads and train tracks. There are also train connections with Brazil and Argentina. Taxis, cars, scooters, and bicycles are the most common means of transportation in the cities; electric trolley and horses and carts are still widely used. About 771 mi. (1,240 km) of navigable waterways provide an important means of transport. There is a ferry service for passengers and vehicles between Argentina and Uruguay. Montevideo is the chief seaport. Pluna, the national airline, provides international air transportation. The main airport is at Carrasco, near Montevideo.

Communication: Some 25 daily newspapers serve the country. The largest dailies are *El País* and *El Día*. Radio broadcasts are devoted to information, culture, religion, commercials, and entertainment. Almost all families own a radio.

Trade: Principal export items are live animals and animal products, vegetables, foodstuffs, beverages, synthetic plastics, hides, skins, textiles, shoes, hats, clay, ceramics, and glassware. Major export destinations are Argentina, Brazil, the United States, Germany, Israel, Italy, the Netherlands, the United Kingdom, France, and Spain. Chief imports are fuels and lubricants, metals, transportation equipment, chemicals, raw material for paper products, rubber, machinery, and appliances. Major import sources are Argentina, Brazil, Germany, Mexico, the United States, and France.

EVERYDAY LIFE

Health: Medical facilities are generally adequate. There is one doctor for every 460 inhabitants. Diseases such as smallpox, yellow fever, and malaria have either been eliminated or are under control.

Education: Education is compulsory for nine years between six and 14 years of age. Primary education begins at the age of six and lasts for six years, and then secondary education lasts for the next six years. Private schools charge tuition and are subject to certain state controls. The University of Montevideo (inaugurated in 1849) is the most prominent institution of higher learning. Public education is free at all levels.

Holidays:

New Year's Day, January 1
Epiphany, January 6
Landing of the Thirty-Three Patriots, April 19
Labor Day, May 1
Battle of Las Piedras, May 18
Birth of General Artigas, June 19
Constitution Day, July 18
National Independence Day, August 25
Discovery of America, October 12
All Souls' Day, November 2
Blessing of the Waters, December 8
Christmas Day, December 25

Housing: People in the cities live generally in apartments or in comfortable single-family houses. Government leaders and other prominent business people live in luxurious high-rise apartment buildings or beautiful mansions. Most homes in the towns have running water. People from lower economic classes such as unskilled laborers, servants, and other people with lower-paying jobs live in tiny shacks on the outskirts of cities. There are far less urban slums than found in other South American countries. In rural areas people live in single-story mud houses. Migrant laborers and ranch workers live in small shacks with thatch roofs and mud floors.

Food: The Uruguayan diet consists mostly of meat (especially beef). The consumption of meat is one of the highest in the world. A typical gaucho meal consists of a mixture of barbecued sausages, kidneys, and strips of beef. Italians have introduced pasta dishes such as spaghetti and lasagna. The national beverage is *yerba maté*, a kind of tea that is traditionally sipped through a straw from a gourd.

Sports and Recreation: Soccer (called *futbol*) is the national and most popular sport. Uruguayan soccer teams were Olympic champions in 1924 and 1928. Soccer and polo games draw large crowds to the city stadiums. Basketball, volleyball, rugby, tennis, cycling, horse riding, show jumping, swimming, surfing, and other water sports are popular. Gaucho rodeos also attract many spectators. Recreation areas of Punta del Este, Lobos Islands for seal colonies, Gorriti Island for superb beaches, and other coastal resorts are visited by thousands of vacationers each summer.

IMPORTANT DATES

1516—The first European person, Juan Díaz de Solís of Spain, lands in Uruguay

1526—Sebastian Cabot, the Italian explorer, sails from Spain

1535—Pedro de Mendoza leads an expedition to the Río de la Plata region

1603—Hernando Arias, the first locally born governor of the Río de la Plata region, sends cattle and horses to the Banda Oriental

1624—The first Spanish colony is established at Soriano

1680—Portuguese soldiers establish the town of Nova Colonia do Sacramento (now Colonia)

1726—Montevideo is founded as a Spanish colony

1750—In a treaty signed in Madrid, Spain agrees to take Colonia from Brazil in return for land from the Jesuit missions

1767—Jesuits are expelled from the Banda Oriental

1776—Colonia is destroyed; Banda Oriental becomes part of the Viceroyalty of the United Provinces of the Río de la Plata

1777—Spaniards attack Colonia and drive the Portuguese out of the country

1806—British capture Buenos Aires from criollos (two months later it is taken back by criollos)

1810—Uruguay declares independence on May 25; Spanish viceroy in Buenos Aires is deposed

1810-14—War of Independence

1811—José Gervasio Artigas launches Uruguay's revolt against Spain

1813—Artigas returns to Banda Oriental to support the Buenos Aires junta

1815—Artigas and his forces return to capture Montevideo

1820—Portuguese troops from Brazil occupy the country

1821—Uruguay is annexed by Brazil

1825—The country is declared independent from Portuguese rule by a group of patriots known as the "Immortal Thirty-Three"; Argentina and Brazil at war

1828—Uruguay becomes independent; after a peace settlement, Uruguay acts as a buffer state between Argentina and Brazil

1830—The first constitution of the new nation is adopted; Uruguay becomes a republic

1832—Charles Darwin visits Uruguay

1835—Manuel Oribe becomes president

1838—José Fructuoso Rivera deposes Oribe as president and installs himself president for the second term

1849—The University of Montevideo is founded

1865—The Colorados gain control with the help of Brazil; War of Triple Alliance in which Argentina, Brazil, and Uruguay are allied against Paraguay

1870—War of Triple Alliance ends with Paraguay's defeat

1914—The Panama Canal is completed

1917—The first constitutional referendum takes place, separating the Catholic church and the state

1939—German ship, the *Graf Spee*, sinks in Río de la Plata

1945—Uruguay declares war on Germany; Uruguay becomes a charter member of the United Nations; the hydroelectric project at Rincón del Bonete is completed on the Negro River

1952 — The presidency is abolished and is replaced by a nine-man council known as the Colegiado with an annually rotating presidency

1958 — In a historic general election the Blancos win power for the first time in the 20th century

1966 — In a national referendum the people vote to abandon the Colegiado and to restore the presidency; the Colorados win a decisive victory and return to office under the leadership of Oscar Gestido; a new constitution comes in force

1967 — Tupamaros launch their insurgency

1971 — Juan Bordaberry is elected president

1973 — The constitution and all political activity are suspended as a civilian-military regime is established

1979 — The Salto Grande Hydroelectric Dam on the Uruguay River is completed

1980 — A new constitution giving military broad authority is rejected in a plebiscite; Treaty of Montevideo establishes the Latin American Integration Association

1981 — Trade unions are legalized (banned since 1973)

1983 — On return to civilian rule, the military initiates talks with the civilian political parties

1984 — General elections are held

1985 — All political prisoners are released and censorship is lifted; Julio María Sanguinetti becomes president

1986 — Legislation is proposed to investigate alleged violation of human rights during the military dictatorship

1988 — A severe drought damages crops and causes deaths of thousands of livestock; a regional summit is held with Argentina and Brazil

1989 — Blanco party leader Luis Alberto Lacalle is elected president; two twenty-four-hour strikes take place in the country

1990 — President Lacalle takes office and launches an economic and social reform program; inflation reaches an all-time high of 128%

1991 — The Southern Cone Common Market, a four-country free trade zone, is created; a Uruguayan journalist, in Iraqi captivity during the Gulf War, is released

1994 — The Mercosur agreement is approved for implementation; the state owned airline Lineas Aereas Paraguayas ceases operations because of debts amounting to $41 million

IMPORTANT PEOPLE

Eduardo Acevedo Díaz (1851-1924), novelist and politician, author of the gaucho novel *Soledad* (1894)

Hernando Arias (1561-1634), Spanish colonist and governor who first sent cattle and horses to Banda Oriental, leading to Uruguay's livestock economy

José Gervasio Artigas (1764-1850), national hero of Uruguay, led the fight for independence against Brazil and Portugal

José Batlle y Ordóñez (1856-1929), Uruguay's most renowned politician, president of Uruguay from 1903 to 1907 and again from 1911 to 1915

José Belloni, Uruguayan sculptor famous for *La Carreta* and *La Diligence* bronze sculptures

Mario Benedetti (1920-   ), contemporary novelist, short-story writer, poet, and essayist

Juan Manuel Blanes (1830-1901), greatest nineteenth-century Uruguayan artist best known for his *Episode of the Yellow Fever*

Juan Bordaberry (1928-   ), president of Colorado party, 1971-1976

Sebastian Cabot (1476-1557), English explorer, navigator, and cartographer

Agustini Delmira (1886-1914), Uruguayan poet

Juan Díaz de Solís (1470?-1516), Spanish navigator, arrived at the estuary of Río de la Plata in 1516

Eduardo Fabini (1883-1951), Uruguay's best-known composer

Pedro Figari (1861-1938), universally acclaimed artist famous for painting vivid scenes of early 20th-century Uruguay

General Venancio Flores (1808-68), Colorado party leader and Uruguayan president, 1852-55, 1865-68

Eduardo Galeano (1940-   ), contemporary Uruguayan writer

José Gamarra, successful contemporary Uruguayan artist

José Hernández (1834-86), Argentine poet, wrote about gaucho life-style in *El Gaucho Martín Fierro* (1872)

Julio Herrera y Reissig (1875-1910), Uruguayan poet, greatest exponent of modernism

Bartolomé Hidalgo, one of Uruguay's most famous poets who wrote about gauchos and their life-style

Juana de Ibarbourou (1895-1979), Uruguayan poet

Luis Alberto Lacalle, president from Partido Nacional (Blanco party) since 1989

Francisco Curt Lange (1903-   ), Latin America's foremost musicologist

Antonio Larreta, Uruguayan author

Colonel Lorenzo Latorre (1840-1916), Uruguayan dictator, 1876-79

Juan Antonio Lavalleja (1786?-1853), leader of the uprising that established Uruguay's independence in 1828

Justus Liebig (1803-73), German chemist, introduced the process of concentrated extract of meat

Francisco Solano López (1827-70), dictator of Paraguay, responsible for the War of Triple Alliance (1865-70)

Ferdinand Magellan (1480?-1521), Portuguese sailor and adventurer

Pedro de Mendoza (1487-1537), Spanish soldier and explorer, founded the first Spanish colony at Buenos Aires (1536)

Carlos Martínez Moreno (1917-   ), Uruguayan author whose most-famous work is *The Wall*

Juan Carlos Onetti (1909-   ), Uruguayan novelist, author of *No-Man's Land* (1942) and *The Shipyard* (1968)

Brigadier General Manuel Oribe (1796?-1857), founder of the Blanco party

Carlos Páez Vilaró, Uruguayan artist, painted a 525 ft. (160 m) mural on the wall of a tunnel connecting two buildings (1960) in Washington, D.C.

Prati, Uruguayan sculptor famous for *The Last of the Charrúa* bronze sculpture

Horacio Quiroga (1878-1937), one of Latin America's foremost short-story writers

Carlos Reyles (1868-1938), Uruguayan novelist

José Fructuoso Rivera (1790?-1854), Uruguay's first president; founder of the Colorado party

José Enrique Rodó (1872-1917), Uruguayan author, one of the most respected defenders of Latin America's cultural traditions whose *Ariel* and *Motivos de Proteo* promotes the idea of the superiority of Latin American culture

Emir Rodríguez Monegal (1921-   ), leading contemporary writer and literary scholar

Juan Manuel de Rosas (1793-1877), Argentine dictator, lived in exile in England from 1852 to 1877

Carlos Sabet Ercasty, distinguished Uruguayan poet

Raúl Sendic (1925-72), leader of the Movement of National Liberation (Tupamaros)

Florencio Sánchez (1875-1910), one of Uruguay's best-known realist dramatists

Dr. Julio María Sanguinetti (1936-   ), Uruguayan president from Colorado party, 1985-90

Joaquín Torres García (1874-1949), famous Uruguayan artist whose style is based on the principles of universalism and constructivism

José Pedro Varela (1845-79), Uruguay's chief education reformer

Javier de Viana (1872-1925), Uruguayan novelist

Bruno Mauricio de Zabala, founder of Montevideo (1726)

José Luis Zorrilla de San Martín, Uruguayan sculptor famous for the statue of *El Gaucho*

Juan Zorrilla de San Martín (1855-1931), known as "the poet of the fatherland," 19th-century romantic poet whose finest work is *Tabare* (1888)

INDEX

Page numbers that appear in boldface type indicate illustrations

About the Author

Newly graduated with a degree in history from the University of Wales, Marion Morrison first traveled to South America in 1962 with a British volunteer program to work among Aymara Indians living near Lake Titicaca. In Bolivia she met her husband, British filmmaker and writer, Tony Morrison. In the last twenty-five years the Morrisons, who make their home in England, have visited almost every country of South and Central America, making television documentary films, photographing, and researching—sometimes accompanied by their children; Kimball and Rebecca.

Marion Morrison has written about South American countries for Macmillan's Let's Visit series, and for Wayland Publishers' Peoples, How They Lived and Life and Times series. Mrs. Morrison also has written *Bolivia, Colombia*, and *Venezuela* in the Enchantment of the World series. Resulting from their travels, the Morrisons have created their South American Picture Library that contains more than seventy-five thousand pictures of the continent.